SUMMERS

SUMMERS

A TRUE LOVE STORY

Best Wishes
Margot Peters
("Jennie")

Edited by

Margot Peters

Library of Congress Control Number:		2011905082
ISBN:	Hardcover	978-1-4568-9712-3
	Softcover	978-1-4568-9711-6
	Ebook	978-1-4568-9713-0

To order additional copies of this book, contact:
Xlibris Corporation
1-888-795-4274
www.Xlibris.com
Orders@Xlibris.com
96937

Silent is the night, long is the road
  Hearts were broken, lost along the way.
  Maybe tomorrow, maybe never,
  But I remembered you today.
  I remembered you today.
     —Lyrics and music by Eric Chesney ©2010

Introduction

In 1948 a sixteen-year-old boy and girl meet briefly, but fatally, on a beach. The boy is so stricken by the girl that he writes her, begging her to answer. "What harm can come from writing letters?" he asks.

The girl replies.

SUMMERS is the story of this boy and girl, based entirely on their letters, which span the years 1948 to 1960. These letters are often funny, sometimes sad, often frustrated and angry. Underneath they are always tender and longing. Finally they are loving.

If bitter-sweet love is your thing: read on.

Thursday, September 15, 1949

Dear Jennie:

Rob Falkner's the name, which means nothing to you at present—however, read on. I'm sixteen, 5'10" tall, a wirey 145 pounds sans garments, and am considered a bright but somewhat erratic student by my tenth grade teachers at Roosevelt High in Des Moines. (A town singularly lacking in charm, but since I've only lived here three months one hopes there may yet be charms to discover.)

To continue the intro: You may recall a day late in August when an uncouth slob named Donald Lindsay attempted to pick you up on the sunny shores of Bradford Beach. Donald was the creep who spilled coke on your movie mag, kicked sand into your potato chips, and burnt a hole in your beach towel in his valiant efforts to make a lasting impression. The quiet, tanned, handsome fellow was, of course, me. Though we never spoke, I'm hoping you may still have a faint memory of the boy who at least did not add to the calamity of your day.

Further info: Somehow, surely by force or theft, Donald wrested your address from you, and I in turn managed to pry it out of him. Donald, you see, is a friend from childhood years in Milwaukee, and I happened to be visiting him those humid days he spent victimizing the bathing beauties of Bradford Beach.

Somehow I doubt that you and Donald are seeing much of one another, and it would sadden me to think that your Photoplay and beach towel were sacrificed for nought. How about accepting me as a "pen-pal" in exchange. You may live to regret it, but then what harm can come from writing letters?

Hopefully, Rob Falkner

*　　*　　*

Sunday, September 25, 1949

Dear Rob,

Strangely enough I do remember a tanned, quiet guy with Donald, but I never expected him to remember me!

Contrary to your assumption, Donald and I have actually been seeing each other. I'm a boarder at Milwaukee Downer Seminary and the headmistress believes that girls and boys should mingle (not too closely, of course), so we exchange monthly dances with St. Johns Military Academy. The first dance was last weekend and Donald was there. Since I wasn't in a swim suit, I doubted he would recognize me, but he came charging across the room the minute I walked in. Are you an especially good friend of his? Why does he go to St. Johns? I get the impression that most boys there are juvenile delinquents.

Donald is now calling three times a week. I don't know much about him except he's persistent.

Actually I live in Wausau. I was visiting my Aunt Marie in Milwaukee when you saw me on the beach. I'm in boarding school because of "problems" at home.

Being in an all girls' school is a new experience for me and I'm going to hate it. I suppose you go to a big highschool? Do you like sports and drinking as much as our mutual friend? I indulge occasionally in the latter, but detest the former. I'm the only girl on the hockey team so far who hasn't scored a goal.

It's nice to get letters in this miserable hovel, so please write soon! Jennie

*   *   *

Monday, October 10, 1949

Dear Jennie:

Hey, thanks for the prompt reply to my letter. I really hadn't expected you to answer at all. I could use a sympathetic soul to "talk" to. Do you mind if I brag about my triumphs, complain about my failures, and cry on your shoulder when I'm blue? Say yes, and you may be letting yourself in for more than you realize.

Let's see if you can take some complaining. I am bored out of my tree at school. Either I'm exceptionally bright, or Theodore Roosevelt High doesn't expect enough from its two thousand students. I'm taking English, geometry to finish my math requirement, swimming to escape gym, world history to avoid sociology, art because I like it, and Latin to please my lawyer father. He admires the Roman legal system so much that he feels his only boy should learn their language. He says Latin will clarify my thinking, develop my values, and give me an appreciation of logic and order. All I know is I'll never learn it at Roosevelt High from our ancient teacher who must be the last surviving Vestal Virgin. However, I believe in doing what I can to keep Dad content. He is already highly skeptical about my interest in art, and very disapproving of what he terms the "artist's life." He thinks that art is simply the means by which I hope to embark on a career of riotous and dissolute living. (For once he is right.)

Roosevelt is a big, impersonal, rich kids school, and I've no close friends as yet. The "in-group" still isn't sure I have the proper credentials, while the "out" group is so big it doesn't need new members. My love life at the moment is particularly bleak. There is a girl with glasses named Gloria who keeps staring at me over her geometry book. At least I think she's staring at me—maybe she's just adrift in a sea of acute and obtuse angles. There is also a "girl next door." Dorothy Jenkins is an unpleasingly plump sophomore. Her mother keeps telling my mother that Dorothy is going to invite me to the first Country Club dance of the season. This news fills my mother with rapture. It fills me with horror.

I'm flattered that you remembered me, especially with Donald so loudly present in the foreground. To help you remember me even better, I'm enclosing a snapshot that my sister Gingy took while I was mowing the lawn. You'll notice jeans instead of bathing trunks, but at least the tanned chest is there for the world's delight.

What is "the problem" that drives you to a nunnery like Milwaukee Downer? I envision scenes of Gothic horror, with you fleeing down the dark corridors of a decaying mansion, pursued by a drunken stepfather, his rabid mastiff, and an insane housekeeper. Surely things like this don't happen in Wausau, Wisconsin!

Hope you will write again. Now you owe me a picture. Remember when you have it taken that I bared my chest for you!

Yours, Rob

*   *   *

Sunday, October 23, 1949

Dear Rob,

'Tis Sunday night and French, Latin, English and Biology stare me in the face. But I shall risk immediate expulsion to answer your most amusing letter.

First of all, how well do you know one of the day girls, Cathy Calloway? I mentioned that I knew two people from Milwaukee, Donald Lindsay and Rob Falkner. The first name made no impression, but yours made her turn a brilliant scarlet, run off down the hall, then run back to ask how well I know you. She still has a terrific crush on you, doesn't she? Confess!

My most fearsome teacher is Miss Main. She rules her Algebra class with an iron fist as she strides up and down the rows, slapping a ruler into her palm. She wears pin-striped suits. The Connecticut license plates on her Ford bear her initials as a sign she hasn't had an accident in thirty years. That type. Advanced Algebra will be my doom. I stay after class erasing wrong answers until my paper is transparent.

Strangely enough, Miss Main is thick with Mrs. Van Wagenen, my English teacher, and the only human being on the faculty. By human, I mean that Mrs. Van Wagenen lives off campus in a home, wears red heels, and appears in plunging necklines at Special Events. She has three children and is interestingly divorced. She actually winks at us lowly students. She calls me "Toots."

Milwaukee Downer isn't exactly a nunnery. All the girls have bulletin boards pinned with photos of boys, pictures of whiskey ads, and college pennants. I've heard more about drinking, smoking, and sex in this "nunnery" than I ever heard at home! But my schedule is fierce:

6:45 rise
7:15 breakfast
8:00 Chapel
8:15 Latin
9:15 English
10:15 Biology

11:15 Study Hall
12:15 lunch
1:15 French
2:15 History
3:15 Algebra
4:15 FREE! FREE! FREE! (unless staying after for algebra)
5:15 study
6:15 dinner
7:00 FREE!
7:30 Study
10:30 LIGHTS OUT!

I know what you mean about "in" groups. I think I'm "on trial." Right away I got elected dorm vice-president, but that was just based on a good first impression. The dorm is very cliquey—seniors pal around with seniors, juniors with juniors. You can tell someone's "in" if they're accepted by the upperclassmen. My friend Robin is accepted by some of the cool seniors which means she's really made it. Oh, boring—this in-out business.

There is only one problem that drove me to this miserable hovel and that is Grandmother.

Donald has been writing three times a week and calling steadily on weekends. Help! He wants to take me out some weekend. So far I have refused. Shall I give in??

It's after eleven and I am writing on my windowsill by moonlight, not a simple task. Your picture now adorns my bulletin board. Please write soon or I shall perish with boredom!

Yours very truly, Jennie

*   *   *

Thursday, October 31, 1949

Dear Jennie,

What a week. Some Milwaukee relatives are visiting and I haven't had two minutes to call my own. I took their daughter Cindy to school as my guest yesterday. I think I'm building up some sort of reputation, for guests are a rare occurrence and this was the second female I had brought to school in two weeks. Speaking of guests, how would you like to visit Des Moines sometime? It's not that far by plane and my parents would be glad to have you. Somehow I think we could have a rare old time.

Are you and Cathy Calloway bosom friends yet? Cathy and I used to attend Mrs. Daley's Dancing School on Friday nights—de rigeur for all children whose parents had social aspirations. Mrs. Daley and her sister Miss Irma tried to instill grace and charm into us, with little success. Your hero Donald was a Daley boy, but he was expelled in disgrace one night when Miss Irma found him shooting craps in the cloakroom during the Grand Right and Left. I always felt sorry for Cathy because she had a face like a pie. I'd ask her to dance during boy's choice because no one else would—besides I owed her. Once Donald stole her "Truth Book" and told me that I was down on her list as "cutest boy" in the class. Such good taste, even in a fat girl, deserves to be rewarded.

"Shall I give in?" you ask. How can I say. I've known Donald since kindergarten. His rich, snobbish Dad owns an engineering firm that Donald is supposed to take over some day. This is dubious, since Donald has yet to master basic addition. His mother tries to be young. His older sister Bitsy graduated from Milwaukee Downer and his younger sister Jean is a brat. That still doesn't answer your question, does it. But be advised: should you give in, I shall wear expression No. 29: insane jealousy.

Later: Our company has finally left and I'm sitting listening to LA BOHEME on the radio, just the romantic notes to put me in the mood to communicate with a mysterious female. (Perhaps I shouldn't admit that I go for this type of music or that I'm currently trying to master Beethoven's "Moonlight Sonata"? If you object I guess I'll have to rush out and start kicking a football around.)

Since you now know the secret of my dark past with Cathy and Donald, what about your Grandmother? I still don't know why a girl from a small lumber town in northern Wisconsin should end up banished to the forbidding halls of MDS.

Write soon, and think seriously about that visit to Des Moines.

Your Iowa admirer, Rob

*   *   *

Saturday, November 12, 1949

Dear Rob,

I'd love to come to Des Moines sometime, but when I asked Elsie (my mother) she wondered whether your parents really want me to visit, or whether it's just you. Somehow she doesn't seem to think that five minutes on Bradford Beach is enough for an invitation to your home, though I've told her we're writing letters. Maybe if your mother wrote Elsie and invited me, she might let me come. I'm wearing expression No. 31 (that's cute!)—doubt mingled with hope. Elsie's address is 1016 Washington Street, Wausau, Wisconsin. I can't come Thanksgiving, but we do have two weeks at Christmas. When is your Christmas vacation?

Right now everyone is longing for Thanksgiving vacation. Every time I hear the Hiawatha train whistle in the distance I want to cry. Even though it's Grandmother's house I have to go back to, I long to flee this miserable hovel.

Last night Donald called and begged me to go to the movies with him because he's on "furlough." I refused, but then his mother called and asked me to go with them. Donald probably had a knife in her back. I'm going tonight—you won't think me too horrible, will you?

Last Sunday we went to the New York Philharmonic Symphony with Stokowski conducting. They played the love music from Tristram and Isolde. I've ordered the record from the music store on Downer Avenue. Mozart, Beethoven, and Rachmaninoff are my favorites, and I play the piano. So you don't have to rush out and kick a football around for me. In fact, please don't—football is so boring!

Anyway, liking classical music is one of the things I don't tell anyone here—they would think I was crazy. Besides, I like popular music too. I think "I Can Dream, Can't I?" is the most beautiful song ever written. Do you?

Cathy Calloway and I have become somewhat friends. She doesn't seem to have much get up and go, but then maybe I have too much? But if she put you at the top of her list, I'd better cultivate her seriously.

I hope tonight won't be too awful!

Your Wisconsin friend, Jennie

P.S. Would you like me to knit you some argyles? All the girls are knitting them.

* * *

Tuesday, November 22, 1949

Dear Jennie:

I was thrilled to hear from your mother that you can come during Christmas. But why do you call her Elsie? If I called my mother Annette, I'd be banished to the basement.

You can set the date. I imagine you'll want to spend Christmas with Grandmother. (You still haven't revealed the mystery, you know.) How about flying? It's definitely the quickest, most enjoyable way. Bring a pair of skates when you come. You do skate, don't you, even though you don't make hockey goals? If there's a good play here I'll try to get tickets. What else would you like to do? How about bringing along some of your piano music? We'll compete.

Dare I ask about the evening with Donald? Dare you tell me?

Yours, Rob

P.S. Of course I'd like some argyles. Two, three pairs, I'm really low on socks.

*   *   *

Saturday, December 3, 1949

Dear Rob,

You write the funniest letters of anybody I've ever known. I got it out of my letterbox right before Algebra and it helped me survive a terrible hour with equations.

I've to take your advice and fly to Des Moines, though I've never flown before. Do you honestly think it's safe, Rob? I can come the day after Christmas if that's all right with you. You haven't told me how long you'd like me to stay. Please consult your parents about this! Downer starts again January 5.

Donald took me to the Downer Theater to see "Sorry, Wrong Number." It was terribly scary, and Donald kept squeezing my hand and acting nervous, though I don't think he was at all. His mother was nowhere in sight! Afterwards was worse. We went to his house and sat in the living room talking to his father. Is Mr. Lindsay a little weird? He asked me all about the McAllister clan, how old our family is, etc. etc. I was terribly embarrassed because I don't know anything about my father. My mother was divorced when I was three, but I didn't like to say that so I made up a terrific bunch of lies. But Mr. Lindsay told me then and there that he hoped Donald and I would marry and reclaim the Lindsay castle in Scotland. Donald seems almost normal by comparison!

I am counting the days until Christmas vacation. Christmas won't be very merry, but since I'm leaving soon after for Des Moines, I don't care that much now.

See you soon! Jennie

* * *

Wednesday, December 11, 1949

Explain yourself!
What is this horrible news? When I came home yesterday the ax fell. There was that awful letter from your mother sending your "regrets." Needless to say I was mildly disappointed. I had such gorgeous plans. We cleaned and painted the recreation room in a big hurry just so we could have a party for you, and I had arranged for skis and play tickets and then I find you're not coming.

I still don't understand what happened. Just because your uncle's coming to Wausau why does that mean you can't come here? Would it be more convenient for you to come the week before Christmas? You're welcome anytime. There's going to be a big fancy formal at the Tromar ballroom the 20th. If you come the first week we can go. You would have the additional thrill of attending my piano recital. For you it would be free. For anyone else it's free too. Occasionally they pay people to fill up the seats.

I don't want to dwell on such an unpleasant subject, but won't you please reconsider? We really should have a few days together to get acquainted, you know. It's hard, realizing that you know that fiend Donald better than you know me. (By the way, his father asked me the same kind of questions, but did not suggest my marrying Donald.)

It snowed this morning. Everything is white and cold. Fine for skiing (gentle hint).

We got our tree tonight. It's a beauty. Wish you could see it (not so gentle hint).

My father, mother, sister, not to mention myself, were looking forward to your visit. If you don't come we shall be crushed.

Please persuade your mother to alter her decision. Or is it really yours.
Disappointed in Des Moines, Rob

*   *   *

Friday, December 13, 1949

Dear Rob,

What are you talking about! Of course I'm coming. I arrive in Des Moines at 10:30 p.m., Tuesday, December 27. I hope that's not past your bed time.

Well, the big Christmas dance has come and gone, and all that's left is a crushed brown gardenia. There was more feuding over that dance than anything in the world—some girls still aren't speaking to each other. I had an okay time because I managed to keep my strapless formal up. Cathy Calloway wasn't there and neither was Donald the Delinquent, thank goodness!

Only fourteen more days till Des Moines! I can hardly wait to slam shut the door of my dorm room and not open it again for 2 weeks.

See you soon, and Merry Christmas. Jenny

*   *   *

Thursday, December 15, 1949

Dear Jennie,

All's right with the world again. At least I think it is. You are coming, aren't you? Today we got a letter from your mother explaining that the letter of refusal was not from her but from your grandmother. Seems your grandmother wrote, using your mother's name. I may be getting a glimmer of the "problem"? Again, why do you call your mother Elsie.

After my last letter you at least know you are welcome. I wish you weren't coming at night, I wanted to get a photo of you alighting on Iowa soil. Hope you're bringing your camera.

I've got three papers due tomorrow. My English teacher Miss Darcy has assigned us eight pages. Why do teachers always pile it on just before vacation? Anyway, I just wanted to let you know the status quo. But please write right away. I won't be easy till I know for sure that you're coming.

Yours, Rob

P.S. I've invited five couples to a party Wednesday evening and if there's snow we'll go on a sleigh ride first. Right now there's a few flakes falling. Pray it snows.

*   *   *

Monday, December 19, 1949

Dear Rob,

I told you Grandmother is evil! What must your mother think? How terrible—first I'm coming, then I'm not, now I am. How can I face your parents!

Well, "Elsie" because one day my mother announced that, since we look more like sisters than mother and daughter, I should call her Elsie from now on. In time I realized that meant Grandmother is my mother.

I'm taking the night plane because there is only one plane per day from Milwaukee to Des Moines and that's it. I'm sorry to keep everyone up so late. I'm not flying from Wausau because my aunt and my mother is afraid of what Grandmother might do. So I'm taking the train back to Milwaukee with my aunt the day after Christmas, and Grandmother thinks I'm staying with Aunt Marie until Downer starts again.

Only one more week. I'm so excited.

Merry Christmas! Jennie

*   *   *

Monday, January 2, 1950

Dear Jennie,

I'm getting this off right away so you'll have a letter Wednesday at school. How was the plane ride home? Did you see the ground at all? Was your aunt there to greet you? Write me all about it.

Sometimes I almost wish you hadn't come—it feels so awful now that you've left. I hope you had at least half as much fun being here as I had in having you. Then at least I know you enjoyed yourself very much. After the plane left I came back home and crawled into bed. I actually fell asleep again and had a wild dream. You were still here singing "I Go to Downer Sem So Pity Me" and I was very happy.

I guess you did a pretty thorough job of packing—the only thing you seem to have forgotten is the dagger pin we found in the antique shop, which I'm returning. Happy hunting. You also left a very nice fragrance of "Magnificence de something or other" hanging in the air of my room. I will have the pictures we took developed Wednesday. And don't despair because they are all of you. What do I want with pictures of myself? I'm as anxious for pictures of you as you are for pictures of me, probably a great deal more.

Must say goodbye now. Have fun at Downer and remember me to Cathy Calloway, Robin, Miss Main, and especially Mrs. Van Wagenen. Do not give my regards to Donald. I'll take care of that myself.

You said you save all my letters. Are you going to save this one too? It certainly is not witty.

All my love, Rob

*   *   *

Friday, January 13, 1950

Dear Rob,

Finally your letter reached me. You sent it by mistake to Wausau. The mailman dropped it on the walk. It was covered by snow, found by the boy who shovels our walk, given to my mother, neglected by her, and finally sent to me in Milwaukee. Poor little letter.

Thank you for one of the most wonderful weeks I've ever had. I only wish it hadn't ended so soon. I enjoyed every single minute, even that last monopoly game I lost so badly! Thank you too for the beautiful pin. It fits nicely into the "ancient" jewel box that we found in that dark antique shop, and I shall keep them both forever to remind me of my wonderful visit.

The trip home was beautiful. The plane headed straight east into the sunrise. At first the sun looked like a red neon sign far below, then it rose higher and higher until the clouds burst into gold and the sun rose in a fiery ball above the mist. Thrilling.

You have the nicest family anyone could hope for, Rob. I just love your mother, father, and Gingy. They're so normal. I know that doesn't sound right, but I mean it as the highest compliment. Anyway, your family was wonderful to me! So were you. And I just love you too.

I dread this long, dreary semester. I don't see how I'll be able to stand four years of college when I could be free in another year and a half. I feel like there are bars on these windows.

Please be sure to send all the pictures. Give your sister Gingy my love and say hello to Dorothy and Jim Gordon for me. I especially enjoyed meeting them.

Love, Jennie

P.S. I wrote Donald suggesting that since it's a new year, that he make a fresh start, stop calling me five times a day and find a new love. He replied that he had always hoped you and I would stay just friends, that he could see it hadn't stopped there, but that he can't give up because he still loves me. Today I received a box of Heineman's chocolates. Our floor wiped it out in three minutes.

*   *   *

Sunday, January 15, 1950

Dear Jennie,

Here are the first pictures. I will send them gradually. They all turned out well. There's an especially good one of you with confetti and streamers in your hair from the New Year's Eve party that I'll send next time.

I too am back at the same old grind—same dumpy school, same vapid teachers, same silly friends, same terrifying subjects, same boring routine day after day. Well, someday we'll be free.

The air of my room still has a faint odor of "Magnificence" hanging about it. I like the smell. How about keeping it near your stationery so your letters will smell of it too.

I've decided we don't write to each other often enough. And I hate this eye for an eye, tooth for a tooth business. Let's just write when we want to without waiting for an answer first.

My junior theme is finished at last. I had planned to polish it off during Christmas vacation, but for obvious reasons did not. Last Thursday I was rudely awakened to the fact that it was due the next day. I dashed home and typed from four p.m. to three-thirty a.m. with fifteen minutes off for supper. Next morning I got up at six and typed until eight. My fingers are still numb, but I finished it. I hope I learned a lesson.

I have been getting letters from Donald too. Somewhere he has gotten the notion that we are carrying on the most scintillating affair. Doesn't he realize that you and I are separated by three hundred and sixty-five miles of rivers, lake, hills, cities, towns . . . . How scintillating can one get?

Jennie dear, I have decided to buy you a birthday present. Whether you decide to send me one for February sixth or not makes no difference. It is more blessed to give than to receive . . . though a pair of hand-knit argyles would be nice.

I don't know what happened to the witty letters you used to rave about. Don't feel witty tonight.

Lots of love, Rob

*   *   *

Wednesday, January 18, 1950

Dear Rob,

I hope this letter doesn't knock you out—I over-doused it with Magnificence de Minuit as I was hurrying for chapel.

Yesterday Robin and I walked down Downer Avenue to a drugstore that has the marvelous hot fudge and pecan sundae. Before we knew it it was four minutes to five. The dorm was SIX LONG BLOCKS away, we'd already been late on Wednesday, we were obviously going to be campused, so we decided to hitchhike. Car after car zoomed by, until finally in desperation we ran alongside a car and it stopped. Our hero! We got a ride back to the Sem but weren't quick enough, so Robin and I don't leave the grounds all next week! Just for five little minutes. Needless to say, I'm bitter. It's also rather awkward, since as a House officer I'm supposed to set a good example.

Last weekend we had a dance with Northwestern. I had bestowed on me a lad by name of Joshua Pericles Sandos. The first thing he said was, "How would you like to come up and see my etchings?" The second was, "Come to the dark room, I'll show you how to develop things." Having got these original thoughts off his chest, he settled down to be more or less of a human being and I had an endurable time.

Mrs. Van Wagenen seems to like me a lot these days and has asked me to lunch next Saturday. I'm honored and of course I'll go.

I'm afraid Cathy's now stuck with our nickname, Cathy Custard. Everyone thinks it's appropriate—she's getting so lazy she simply waddles onto the basketball court and tosses the ball in any direction. Whereas I, like on the hockey field, am a real pistol.

I dream about the week in Des Moines. I wish I weren't such a sentimentalist. It hurts sometimes.

Say hi to Gingy for me and give your mother my love . . . and take a lot for yourself too. I think it's a wonderful idea to write whenever we want as long as you make it often. You can't possibly like my poor letters as much as I love yours.

Jennie

P.S. Jim Gordon wrote me, at least the letter had his signature. But I doubt he wrote it because he asked me whether Downer was strict. Surely he gathered that from what I said at the party.

*   *   *

Sunday, January 22, 1950

Dear Jennie,

I wasn't too surprised to hear that Jim Gordon wrote you. Rita says he has a big crush on you. Oh, you little old enchantress, you. Dorothy Jenkins came over the other night and said, "I think Jennie is just as darling as she can be." This is a definite departure for Dorothy as she never admits that anyone is darling but herself. Do not let all this go to your head.

Sorry you can't leave the grounds for a week. How about spending the extra time writing me letters.

Your mother wrote mine a letter today. She said she was so happy you could come to Des Moines and get away from the ultra—sophisticated atmosphere of Downer. I guess she's afraid you're getting too worldly. Better not send her that photo of you in the gold and black cocktail dress.

I am now more or less firmly entrenched in my new classes and have a singularly fierce schedule and some singularly fierce teachers. For Miss Brady the life of a teenager revolves around English. The quantity of assignments makes quality impossible. What's worse, we are now studying an extremely dismal period of English literature and I simply cannot focus. While Miss Brady is extolling the glories of Anglo-Saxon literature to her enthralled class, I am 230 pages and 700 years further into the book communing with the witticisms of Alexander Pope. Have you read "The Rape of the Lock"? It has its moments—"This lock the muse shall consecrate to fame, and 'midst the stars inscribe Belinda's name."

I received a "gangsta" kodacolor of Donald the other day, replete with gin bottle, cigarette, guns, rumpled clothes and that Little Caesar look. Wouldn't hurt his feelings by laughing for the world.

This must be all for now. Please write very soon.

Love, Rob

*   *   *

Saturday, January 28, 1950

Dear Rob,

I have just returned from lunch at Gimbels with Mrs. Van Waganen. I thought I'd be home by 2:30, but it's now past four! She is certainly interesting, about 38 (?), has two daughters, and though she teaches French and Spanish, is working on a degree in psychiatry. Some of the students find her magnetic, others think she is a sorceress and a show-off. I don't know what to think, but she's a very warm and witty person. I'm beginning to think she may like me too much, though? Several times during lunch she covered my hand with hers and gazed at me with a most meaningful expression. I wonder if Freud's got a special complex for teachers—he ought to.

This miserable hovel had a scandal a few days ago. A junior who needed help with her homework went down to first floor and knocked at Miss Parker's door. She thought she heard someone say "Come in." There was Miss Parker in bed with the music teacher, Mrs. Gold! Barbara said she just stood there, eyes bulging, then turned tail and ran. Naturally she told all second floor and that same night we had a bull session in her room to talk about it. Most of us were pretty shocked, but a couple of seniors argued that they didn't see anything wrong with two women making love because after all, only a woman knows what a woman wants!

I debated a long time about telling you this, Rob. You'd better burn this letter so your family won't read it. Anyway, I think one reason Mrs. Van Wagenan may like me is that I'm flip with her, whereas most of the girls bow down.

I've been staying with Aunt Marie ever since my last exam on Thursday. Biology was a terror past description. Miss Brady may be your downfall, but biology is mine.

I feel I should warn you that if you don't receive your birthday present exactly on time, don't despair. YOU WILL GET IT! By the way, do you want me to call you for your birthday? Of course, I'd probably have to reverse charges. I'm down to my last penny.

Please write me about Mrs. Van Wagenan. I wish I could talk it over with you. Robin says, "She probably just has a very strong interest in your welfare." Love, as always, Jennie

* * *

Tuesday, February 7, 1950

Dear Jennie,

Sometimes I wonder whether your aunt realized when she sent you to Downer that she was incarcerating you in a den of iniquity. But I'm glad you told me, and I'm hardly shocked, though I might have been if you'd said you jumped in with Miss Parker and Mrs. Gold. I have read "Well of Loneliness," you know. Besides, I've known Donald a long time. A teacher at one of his private schools used to soap the locker room floor on Saturday nights and photograph the boys sliding around on their bare bottoms. Can't imagine why anyone would want a picture of Donald's rear end. I suppose this little episode of yours was along this line. Perhaps you'd better lock your door.

But I don't quite understand what you were saying about Mrs. Van Wagenan. I thought that last semester you were "madly in love" with her and would have given anything for her to feel the same way. I'd like to talk this over with you too. Freud undoubtedly would chalk it up to suppressed sex instincts in babyhood. Is Mrs. Van Wagenan simply too friendly for a teacher? Tell me more.

About your phone call. I half-heartedly expected you to call yesterday on my birthday. When you didn't I gave up hope. Tonight I was preparing to dash off to a Civic Music Concert with Gloria (you remember Gloria) when the phone jangled. Gingy thought the call was for my mother, who was dressing for the PTA meeting. Finally it became clear that the call was for me, so zipping myself together with one hand I grabbed for the phone with the other. Could you make any sense out of what I said? The connection was terrible. Besides, there was much disturbance at this end. Gingy stood there gaping at me as I stood there shouting at you. I'm sorry it didn't turn out better—there was so much I wanted to say. Next time call collect so we can take our time. Also it would be nice if you could get me alone. What were you saying about Donald? Mrs. Van Wagenan? Grandmother? Despite everything, it was really great to hear your voice again. Thanks for calling!

Miss Darcy is leaving to get married and the girls took up a farewell present collection. I suggested a black lace nightgown, but no one else seemed enthusiastic and the class decided on an electric frying pan. Today we had a farewell party in class. Miss Darcy cried, the girls cried, and I myself was not above a pang or two. We're decidedly worried about who might replace her. We may have to stow the cards and start writing again.

Have you heard more from Jim Gordon?

I'm beginning to see double and the typewriter ribbon is sticking. Besides, I'm da—tired, so I think I'll turn off the light and lie down to pleasant dreams—of you? Probably not. I never seem to dream of what I'd like to.

Much, much love, Rob

*   *   *

Thursday, February 9, 1950

Dear Rob,

I'm sorry too we didn't have a better connection, but I probably said nothing you would regret having missed. You know, it's funny—I've never thought of telephoning you, yet all we'd have to do to hear each other's voices is pick up a receiver and dial! My allowance would cover some calls to Iowa. But how can I possibly guess when you would be alone? You might strike out on your own and call ME when you have the urge, the time, and the money.

Mrs. Van Wagenan is very interesting, I agree. First I'd better explain that when I say I'm madly in love with someone, I just mean a kind of crush. That's what I meant last semester when Mrs. Van Wagenan certainly was my favorite teacher. But now she seems to come at me with a great deal of enthusiasm. Worse, she's become overly sensitive. The other day when she mentioned she would be getting her degree in psychology this summer, I quipped, "O god, the blind leading the blind!" The kind of thing I always say, but this time she got up and left the table. Rob, I don't know what to do. She seems to go out of her way to run into me in the halls, then won't look at me. I need advice. This only for you and Robin.

This weekend is St. John's Midwinter—everyone bundles into the Downer bus and drives to Delafield singing dirty songs all the way, chaperones loudest of all. Two days of tobogganing, skating, dancing (official) and heavy necking. I've been invited by someone named Clare Reese and Robin will be with her boyfriend Page Barker. The thought of Donald lurking does not cheer me.

Today was a most beautiful day—54 degrees and everything melting. Robin, Sandy and I took a walk during gym class and headed for the lake. The big ice chunks have drifted far out from shore and the water was a cold brilliant blue. Oh, the pull from now until June will be so long and if spring doesn't come soon, I'll die.

Have to confess I'm beating weeds—off campus, of course. We sneak down (hopefully) deserted alleys after school. Who knows, Miss Main the Pain may be lurking. We cuff weeds as we walk. Robin's are a perfect tatter of burns and I've drastically singed the camel's hair coat that Elsie paid her last sou for. How can I go home at Easter! Downer boarders are campused for a month if caught smoking off—campus, expelled if caught in their rooms. Pray for me!

Must stop. Tomorrow I will fully realize the terror of not having done my French. I don't care now.

What is "Well of Loneliness"?

Much love to you, Jennie

P.S. I did get a letter from Jim Gordon the other day, hardly up to the usual Des Moines standard. I may answer if I have time. All I remember is a tall boy with red hair, maroon shirt and yellow tie. Remember wondering if he was colorblind.

P.P.S. Guess what! I'm almost positive you'll soon be receiving a gorgeous pair of red, navy and yellow argyles, your birthday present, remember? But please rush me your sock size—I can't just keep going forever. The next time I see you, I expect you to be wearing them, even on Bradford Beach in July!

* * *

Thursday, February 16, 1950

Jennie, Jennie—

A fire on one end, a fool on the other. Beating weeds? I thought you had more sense. Do you really want to be campused for months and forego the ecstasies of St. Johns and lunches with Mrs. Van Wagenan? Cease and desist.

Speaking of life's unsavory side, I heard from Donald today. He informed me that he had spent his weekend pass at the Empress Burlesque House in Milwaukee. That seemed natural, but then he castigated the Empress as a lowdown, vulgar and lewd place he'd never enter again. If Donald thinks something is lowdown and vulgar, the Empress must be unspeakable.

Here is another picture of you. And from me those are all you're going to get, honey—pictures of you. Simple fact is, I didn't take any of myself. The only pictures of me are the ones on your film. I hope they're better than the last. There is a boy in my homeroom who looks exactly like I do on that picture—always smiling, eager to please, friendly, but well, you know.

You will accuse me of sounding like Aunt Marie, but personally I think you're making mountains out of molehills as far as Mrs. Van Wagenan is concerned. Middle course, middle course. Just because you don't love her with a mad passion doesn't mean you have to avoid her. Can't you be friendly without going to extremes? I wouldn't make any more caustic cracks since she's obviously no longer taking them well, but I still think you're exaggerating the situation. Why must you be either a bosom pal or an enemy. Actually, I'd love to meet her. I like older people.

My sock size is eleven and a half, I asked my mother. I'm not, however, going to worry excessively about suffering heat prostration from wearing argyles in July. Nor do I expect that sweater you started for me in Des Moines any time in the near future. If I were to appear in the knitted wear you promised me, I'd be the best dressed man west of the Mississippi. If I were to appear in the knitted wear you've sent me, I'd be run in for indecent exposure.

What gave you the idea that Jim Gordon has red hair? Gordon has dark hair, crew cut and a rather subdued taste in clothes. Have you answered his letter? I went skating the other night and he came for me with such enthusiasm that I thought I must have done some dastardly thing to offend him. But no, he only wanted to chat about you. Are you thrilled to learn he's still fond of you? I am not.

I will close with a little phrase you are going to be seeing a lot of. It took me 45 minutes with the aid of a French-English dictionary to concoct the thing, and I am going to get my money's worth.

Vous avez tout mon amour, Rob

*   *   *

Sunday, February 19, 1950

Dear Rob,

Thank you so much for the valentine. I think of you too "not more than 24 hours a day, 365 days a year."

Guess who dropped in on me yesterday in the student lounge to spend the afternoon? Donald's sister Bitsy, and Donald. I felt faint and backed out of the room. But Donald made a scene and commanded his sister to make me come and talk to him. Forcing myself to assume Expression No. 23—frozen smile of politeness—I sat down and actually managed to carry on a vice-free conversation for two or three minutes. The rest of the hour he packed so full of vice, sin, and corruption that episode he doused the tiny flame of hope still burning in my ever-tolerant heart.

I suppose you're right about Mrs. Van Wagenan, though I can't help feeling that I've underestimated the situation. Last Sunday, for instance, was a gray old day and some of us got into a game of hide and seek in the school building. Sandy and I, pursued by Robin, dove into Mrs. Van Wagenan's room, slammed the door, and turned around to see—Mrs. Van Wagenan! Laugh, but I was terrified, especially when she ordered me to stay behind under pretense of showing me some old test scores. And you think I'm making too much of the whole thing. Okay, nothing happened, and yet it did.

I've been caught! Remember those kitchen raids and room parties I've told you about? Well, last Tuesday night I went into Robin's room and we talked, talked—I guess a bit too loudly. Anyway Mrs. Holmes, the floor mother, came charging in with the witty comment, "Since when, Miss Wrezin and Miss McAllister, is this a double?" We were convicted WITHOUT TRIAL and sentenced. If when you next see me my hands are rough and red, remember the months I've scrubbed the lavatory and overlook.

So Jim Gordon has dark hair and a crew cut? That's funny. Then who was the red-head?

Today Sandy and I went for a hike through Lake Park. As we paused under the bridge for a cigarette (afraid I'm still beating weeds), some boys approached with cans of Schlitz. Assuming our most beguiling expressions, we offered to buy the four cans for 50 cents a piece. To our surprise they took us up on it—nay, offered to deliver a case of the stuff to the same spot next Sunday for $4 dollars. Bargain struck and we have a rendezvous in Lake Park a week from today at three o'clock. Aimez-vous le beer? I kind of don't.

Last night I dreamed I was sleeping in your bed in Des Moines and your mother came to wake me. Immediately I burrowed under the covers saying, "Please let me stay, I don't want to go back to Downer."

Tu as tout mon amour aussi, Jennie

* * *

Tuesday, February 28, 1950

Dear Miss McAllister:

Ever since I first glimpsed you lolling on Bradford Beach I have been a fan. I admire your wit, sincerity, and beauty—qualities so few people possess. I just had to write and tell you how I adore you and wish you every success. Your loyal admirer for life, Rob Falkner.

The above, with a few alterations, is the type of letter that used to net me autographed portraits of Barbara Stanwyck, Esther Williams, and Betty Grable when I was a star-struck lad. Do you suppose it is worth one or two of the small pictures you took while you were here in Des Moines? I am enclosing another picture, but only to prove that I am confident that you will send me the 8x10 you owe me. If at the moment you are low on funds, kindly send me the negatives and I will develop the prints myself.

Reading your last, a couplet springs to mind:

> Once Downer girls were white as snow,
> But that was a helluva while ago.

Everything seems to go wrong. For one thing, the Regional winners in the Art Contest were announced. The winners get a gold key as a symbol of their artistic achievement and a FREE DINNER. I had eight entries in the show and they hung six of them, but the judges, obviously hostile to real talent, did not pick one of them. I am livid with rage. I am going to crash the awards dinner anyway, if only to thumb my nose at the misguided judges. But the idea of having to pay for my dinner while lesser lights eat free sets me fuming. If unrecognized in '51, I shall go down to the show with a knife and slash everything to ribbons.

So much for my artistic life. Now to my social. You remember Gloria? By some means I must rid myself of her menacing shadow. Many moons ago she asked me, looking so innocent that I never guessed she was a harbinger of doom, what I was doing the night of March 18. I said "Nothing," and let it drop. The next thing I knew she announced that I was taking her to a fancy formal that night. Since Gloria is tottering on the brink of madness, I couldn't flatly refuse since that might give her just the push needed to send her plummeting into the abyss. So I let the matter ride and prayed for Divine Intervention. Then came the straw that broke the camel's back. Martha called and asked me to take her. Now whereas compared to you Martha is dull and drab, compared to Gloria she is lively, attractive, vivacious, and charming. Besides, I like Martha. But naturally I had to express my regrets, so it really looks like I shall be dancing with Gloria. The very thought of holding her in my arms!—her touch is the kiss of death. Maybe I can break the whole thing off before the 18th without being too cruel. I'm going to try.

You know what I think of cigarettes. Beer I can drink, Schlitz not Pabst.

Whatever happened to the argyles that were "almost finished"? Please don't run down to Gimbel's or Chapman's. They must be the work of your own precious little hands.

Tu as tout mon amour, encore, Rob

*　　*　　*

Friday, March 10, 1950

Sweetest Rob,

You have no right to threaten me for not sending pictures until you send me the long promised one of yourself. To affirm your trust in me, however, I enclose a photo.

Much has happened since I last wrote. The Sophmore dance has come and gone, Donald came and went, some Northwestern boys waltzed in and out, and the flu has come and stayed. Donald called on me last Friday, and we actually talked about some serious things, you among them. Donald says he is very worried about you, but thinks that if left alone, everything will straighten itself out in your confused mind. I think perhaps it's Donald who's confused, although I must admit he opened up a sinister train of thought. Tell me you aren't passionless!

I fear I don't sympathize with you about a lost night with Gloria. Really, Rob—when a girl asks if you're free for a night, she's not going to say, "Well, I'm not" and walk away. I think your conduct thoroughly wishy-washy, and cruel as it sounds, I feel you deserve your fate.

Our Sophomore Dance was a huge success. Afterwards we drove out to the Pig 'n Whistle, stocked up on barbeques, drove to the lake, sang songs, tried dancing to keep warm, got sleepier and sleepier, finally gave up the idea of watching the sun rise, and staggered to my aunt's (I had taken an overnight). The next morning we went to Lake Park and made snowmen in the snow that had fallen overnight. My levis got so wet that they froze on me, and that is how I got the flu, a temperature of 103, was delirious Sunday night, called the nurse who was struggling to get aspirins down my throat a B—h (well, she is), and got reported to the house mother.

I'm really surprised you didn't place in the art contest. How blind can judges be! But don't be discouraged, Rob, there's always next year.

I wish I'd taken art this semester, I'm sorely in need of A's right now. I finally pulled a B in biology, but geometry, I'm afraid, is going to be a C. My English teacher told me the other day that I write like Virginia Woolf. Who is she?

Must go. Here is a new phrase for you—

Je te donne mon esprit, mon coeur et ma vie, Jennie

*   *   *

Tuesday, April 4, 1940

Dear Neglected, but not forgotten,

Why haven't you answered my last six letters? Could it be because I never wrote them? Every morning I said, "Today I will write to Jennie," every night crawling into bed I said, "Tomorrow I will write to Jennie." I don't know why, but I have the egotistical idea that you suffer tortures waiting for letters that never come. Perhaps that's because I suffer tortures when you don't answer promptly. I don't suffer quietly either, but go cursing, raving and stomping about the house.

Where is that picture you were going to send to affirm my trust in you? YOU FORGOT TO ENCLOSE IT. My trust is sorely shaken.

Even though, heartless wretch, you don't sympathize with me, I will tell you about my lost evening with Gloria. I gave her a corsage of baby iris which she thought were orchids, so her evening got off to a rousing start. We immediately tied up with another couple of misfits. Then Gloria asked me to dance. Then we danced again and again and again. Gloria had to dance EVERY DANCE. This simply isn't done. What's worse, she discovered they had rigged up a bunch of balloons on the ceiling to drop down on the dancers unexpectedly. She was determined to have a balloon, so we had to dance all evening in a space of two square yards directly under the balloons. By the end of the evening when the balloons were loosed, the floor beneath them was a good deal worn. However, Gloria got a balloon and I gave her my balloon, which made her intensely happy. All in all it wasn't the nightmare I expected. I tried to give Gloria a good time and I think I succeeded. However, we have begun to drift apart of late. I'm taking it very hard. Crushed is the word. Shed a tear for me, shed a tear.

Well, my dear, I must begin "Macbeth." Today Miss Brady announced that we would dramatize certain acts. I happen to be Macbeth, with a 34-line soliloquy which I must deliver in such a way as to put Maurice Evans to shame. "I go and it is done, the bell invites me. Hear it not Duncan; for it is a knell, Which summons thee to heaven or to hell."

Exeunt and good night.
Je te donne mon esprit, mon coeur et ma vie. Aussi. Rob

Dare I say "Write soon?"

*   *   *

Wednesday, April 12, 1950

Dear Rob,

I am just this minute back from Rockford and Sandy's house. Did I tell you I was invited to Sandy's for spring vacation? When we stepped on that Rockford-bound train, Sandy and I really cut loose. We beat two packs of weeds before I got deathly sick in the lavatory.

However, I did pull myself together enough to down two Dacharies before we reached the station. We were met by a whole carload of kids and whisked off to Sandy's house where a big party was in full swing. First question I was asked was, "Do you French kiss?" Took my breath away. Then we all went swimming in her outdoor heated pool. I'll send you pictures from the Rockford rag. Next day we bummed around in Sandy's convertible picking up boys. That night there was a barbeque by the pool. Colored lights, warm spring night, soft music, a handsome boy—what more could I ask for? You? Well, anyway, it was a wild, happy time and I hated returning to the old prison.

Rob, Rob, I'm in a most restless mood. I can hardly wait to get out of school and get married. I want a house with forest green walls and white rugs. But all I really want is to get out of here. Please write me soon. I suppose this sounds totally insane, but it is just the way I feel. And a geometry test tomorrow.

Did I tell you that I had to crawl out of the infirmary to go to Sandy's? Craziest thing trying to convince the nurse I wasn't sick with a temperature of 102. They wanted to keep me there over spring vacation! My temperature must be closer to 120 now. Feel ghastly.

Write soon—the minute you get this. Please.

Love and other indoor sports, Jennie

*   *   *

Friday, April 14, 1950

Jennie:

I feel fatherly tonight. Just bursting with advice. One piece is to forego the clever Downer endings to your letters. Save them for Jim Gordon or the Rockford boys. Another is to forego even slightly some of the cigarettes, some of the boys, and some of the wild times. I'd better keep the rest to myself, I suppose. You probably don't care for me in a fatherly mood. Or do you?

Still restless? Still panting to get out of school so you can dash off and get married? Who are you going to marry, the milkman?

I still haven't decided whether I'll marry five times or be a bachelor. The reason for the vast contrast is that I think I am too restless to be a good husband. Either the girl would never marry me, or we wouldn't get along and I'd have to find another. One thing I do know: I couldn't bear to be tied down to a normal, routine—like the one my parents live who you admire so much. I would rather be poor and have a strange and exciting life than be a slave to convention or routine.

I hope by now that you are fully recovered. Why don't you slow down, Jennie? You're trying to live too much too fast.

Send the pictures the newspaper photographer took at Rockford. I can take it. I am surprised at how much I miss you. Really. We must get together sometime. This summer? That sounds so far away, though. Sixty-seven days or something like that. A lifetime.

Write soon, that's SOON, Rob

*   *   *

Jeudi, le 20 Avril, 1950

Dear Rob,

The implications of your last letter leave much to be desired. "We must get together sometime." Oh, really. Yes, we must, mustn't we. Sometime when I'm not too busy. Say in a year or so. Take this as a bitter thrust.

Don't know who I'll marry. Surely not the milkman. I have thought of you, but the prospect of being one of five wives doesn't cheer me. Perhaps after all I'll have a career and forego the whole business. Or perhaps I won't. It's just that everything now seems stale and childish. Enough of inane speculation!

Guess what! I'm almost finished with your ski sweater. It's black and white with maroon. It was supposed to be a surprise, but I couldn't wait to tell you. Are you pleased? Of course, I expect something in return. (Right now wearing Expression No. 53: inward amusement.)

This isn't much of a letter, but write soon, please.

Love, Jennie

P.S. I like you in a fatherly mood. I never had a father, not really.

PP.S. Enclosed are the Latin translations I promised you last Christmas. I hope they're not too late.

*   *   *

Thursday, April 27, 1950

Darling!

How kind of you to send the Latin translations. I had given up all hope of seeing them. I hope I don't sound ungrateful if I tell you that we have long left Caesar's Gallic Wars and are currently into Cicero. But I treasure them, nevertheless.

In English Miss Brady is making us read and outline two short stories a night. It takes all my time but I kind of enjoy it. I have found some fascinating stories by Dorothy Parker. Have you ever read "But the One on the Right" or "The Little Hours?" In the former I found a new French expression. Vin triste. Let's go out and get vin triste sometime, huh?

I gather from the implications of your last letter that mine are too casual for you. But I didn't say "sometime"—I said "this summer." I think that's quite different.

I hope you won't think me a hateful old cynic, love, if I do not go into raptures over my ski-sweater until I see it. Of course, I'm sure I will see it, but how can I go skiing with bare feet? The argyles, remember? And so help me, if I see Jim Gordon in a black and white and maroon ski sweater—. Actually I know that I will eventually be the rage of the ski trails in the sweater, and certainly I will do something for you in return. Name it. (I am wearing Expression No. 53.)

Have been taking vocational guidance tests. I got a 3% in mechanical ability, 3% in social work, and 5% in computation. I got a 96% in artistic and literary, 91% in musical, and 88% in persuasive skills. I don't know what can be deduced from the questions they ask. "Would you rather play hide-and-seek with a bunch of cretins, or play the piano?" If the fact that I'd rather play the piano than hide-and-seek means I'm cut out to be a musician, that's all right with me.

Have just finished "Hamlet" and "A Midsummer Night's Dream" at the gentle insistence of Miss Brady. Found the former without thrills, the latter delightful—in fact it's my favorite Shakespeare. I had heard the rumor about the relationship between Hamlet and his mother, but though I read carefully, not a trace of "damnèd incest" could I find. I suspect the nicest thing was started by a group of English teachers to make sure their students would read the play.

No more tonight.

Much love, Rob

*   *   *

Friday, May 5, 1950

Dear Rob,

I've lost 12 pounds, probably because I have been wasting away in the infirmary for half the semester with I don't know what. I look like somebody's dead sister.

We had a house dance last Friday and Jack Rees from St. Johns came. I have decided that the reason I like him is because he seems to loves me, which is gratifying. Of course, I have only one side of me in common with him. The side that loves dancing, dacheries, night clubs, smoky dark restaurants where they serve wonderful french-fried lobster—things like that. In common with you I have our love of art, piano, movies, books, records, and a general ability to have so much fun together that the rest of the world goes away. I guess it's pretty obvious which things are the most lasting.

I enclose one day's supply of the little blue slips I get when Donald calls just to show you what my life has been like ever since spring vacation. Vera, the maid, gets a charge out of Donald. I don't.

Something awful happened the other day, to put it mildly. Our headmistress is Nar Warren Taylor, six feet tall and just as mean. Well, I found a note in my letterbox saying she wanted to see me after classes. Of course I was in a total panic all day. Four o'clock finally came and I dragged myself down the hall to her office. Her secretary, Mrs. Rohn, gave me a big smile that didn't make me feel better. We call her "Peaches Rohn" because she's always saying, "Isn't that peachy!" It wasn't peachy. Nar Warren, looking like the "Ring of the Niebelung," told me she could not approve the renewal of my scholarship for next year. It seems that the maximum number of demerits for a student in good standing is 15—and I have 35! I blubbered that I'd worked off at least 100 demerits staying after school in study hall, but it seems that doesn't really count. Oh, I don't want to go into it, but I cried and cried. All I could think was how horrible facing Wausau and Grandmother is going to be. Since you like older women I suppose you're far more sympathetic to Nar, but the way she reached for a kleenex box from her top drawer—as though she'd done it before and would do it a hundred times again—was inhuman!

Anyway, I'm out, banished. And I'm too ashamed to tell anyone, so I just go around pretending I'll be back next year. I haven't even told Robin or Sandy, and I don't think I can. Sandy and I are supposed to room together next year—we even got dibs on the best double on second, the corner room everyone dies for. Oh, Rob, what am I going to do? Aunt Marie knows, and I have received seven letters because, though she's only a few blocks away, she refuses to call. And of course, Elsie knows, but since she's always on my side, that doesn't count. Anyway, what I plan to do, is just to go through the rest of the year as best I can. I don't think I told you, but for graduation every senior has a junior flower girl. My favorite senior picked me for her flower girl—but she doesn't know! Wish I could die right now.

No more tonight. I'm sure you'll understand.

Excruciating love, Jennie

P.S. Mrs. Van Wagenan asked me to lunch this Saturday! Miss Main calls her Miggy.

*   *   *

Wednesday, May 10, 1950

Dear Jennie,

Have I missed something along the line? Who is this Jack Rees who "seems to love you"!

Since Aunt Marie has written you seven letters on the subject of you're not returning to Downer next year, I'm sure you don't want one from me. Would you consider me a heartless cad if I say that your being in the infirmary most of the semester—exaggeration though I know it is—alarms me far more than your not returning to Downer next year? Downer may be the scholastically superior school you assure me it is, but on the unscholastic side, anyone reading your letters were think you were attending a school for juvenile delinquents. O.K., that's a bit strong, but you get the point. My diagnosis of all your problems has been TOO MUCH DOWNER.

In one thing you do have all my sympathy, and that is going back to live with Grandmother. You still haven't revealed the dark secret, but the sinister hints you've dropped make me shudder for you, darlin'. Why do you have to live with her? Your mother has a job. Why can't you just move out?

Now a big question. Every year friends invite us to use one of their cottages at Delavan Lake for a few weeks, and this year we'll be in residence June 9-July 1. How about running out and visiting for a week? It's not far from Milwaukee, you know. You are hereby invited. Let me know. There's going to be a shortage of kids this year, I need someone to keep me company, and I can think of no one that's better company than you. They have a stable there full of horses and you could teach me how to ride. The swimming is wonderful. We have riots going to the movies. It is beautiful (and romantic) to sit on the pier and watch the moon rise.

On a slightly different subject, what do l'envoi, faut de mieux, rondeau redouble, and vers demode mean? I love Dorothy Parker but since she is always throwing in French I must resort to you for help. This is important, believe me. I'm doing a major theme on Dorothy Parker, and since I must discuss the theme of every poem it will help if I know what they mean.

His ways are not the wicked ways
He's not the like of you.
He treads the path of reckoned days,
A sober man and true.

He's none to kiss away my mind—
A slower way is his.
Oh Lord! On reading this I find
A silly lot he is.

I thought of this as I read that list of things that I have in common with your better side. Books, music, literature, movies, art. I realize you were being very serious, but the way you put it struck me as very funny. Really, sweetheart, how did you and I ever manage to have such fun? Apropos, have you ever seen Donald's picture entitled "Sacred and Profane Love?" He has it in his bedroom. Maybe he'll show it to you—but in the living room, please.

You must tell me all about lunch with Mrs. Van Wagenan. Does this mean you are blissfully reconciled?

Please note: I am going to telephone you on your seventeenth birthday. I don't suppose there's a chance of finding you alone and unoccupied, but I'm going to try.

I hope your mother will say you can come to Delavan. Have I coaxed you enough, or shall I try again? You are welcome anytime after June 10.

Dear Jennie, what is "excruciating love?" I don't know, do you?

All sorts of love, excruciating included, Rob

*   *   *

Thursday, May 18, 1950

Dear Rob,

Thank you for calling! I'm sorry I didn't sit down immediately and write like I promised, but fifty things came up that evening, among them two happy birthday calls from Donald. Please be assured that I have never entered Donald's bedroom—and never will. Though sometimes I wonder bleakly whether his sheer persistence will finally break me down. You know, marrying him just so he won't call and write so much.

I pray I can come to Delavan. I wrote my mother a pleading letter, but Rob, have you asked your mother? (This sounds familiar.) How do I get to Delavan? Downer gets out June 12 and I could stay with Aunt Marie for awhile, I think. Will you really let me teach you to ride? How I would love it if you would! But first how do I get there? Details, please!

The phrases you asked about are as follows: l'envoi—dispatch, message; faut de mieux—for lack of better; vers demode—toward destruction. Rondeau redouble I can't find. I think rondeau is a round or verse, and I think redouble means "redoubled," but it doesn't make sense, does it?

I didn't mean to sound so stupid about the things we share. But come to think of it, I don't quite understand how we manage to have so much fun. Everything drab somehow becomes magical and funny—even going to the grocery store is an adventure. That sounds silly, but it's true.

I didn't go to lunch with Mrs. Van Wagenan after all. I couldn't sit there smiling and pretending I'd be back next fall and I didn't have the courage to admit the truth. I spent my last shekels buying her some perfume and enclosed a note wishing her a good summer. Just this minute it occurs to me that of course she knows everything! She probably asked me to lunch to comfort me.

Why don't we "just move out" you ask? I wish I knew. Elsie earns a pittance, even though she's now the society editor on the Wausau paper, but I don't think that's the reason. She's talked about moving out for as long as I can remember. We've even sneaked away to look at apartments. Once we actually looked at a house with a fireplace. But nothing ever happens. No one talks about things in my family. I still don't know why my mother and father got divorced. I remember once when I was five at the Fair with my grandmother, we met my father on the midway and she yanked me away and wouldn't let me talk to him. She hates him, but I don't know why, and I don't know why we can't move. I think she has some kind of power over my mother.

Less than thirty days, and I may see you again. Please tell your mother to write mine. And if she gets a reply written in slanted old—fashioned writing instead of small and round, it's from Grandmother not Elsie!

Loads of love, Jennie

P.S. Enclosed is my junior picture. I hope you like it.

*   *   *

Sunday, May 28, 1950

Dear Jennie,

Thank you so much for the photo. It is so beautiful. Really. You look so young, sweet, and so innocent I could—never mind. I've decided to relax my anti-vice crusade. You may smoke your precious Pall Malls at the lake to your heart's content. And I like you so much better minus the bangs. Of course Gingy asked if that was bubble bath around your shoulders, but don't worry about her foolish notions. It wasn't bubble bath, was it?

The other day Miss Wheeler told her Art class that she needed five of her most skilled pupils to help with the Des Moines Art Center Membership Drive. It seems we had to sit and paint in the largest window of Younkers Department Store. (You remember Younkers.) The idea was that a crowd would gather and become inspired by our daubing to support the Center. The great day arrived and the five eager artists piled into a 1933 Ford with Mrs. Wheeler, who is very large, and paint boxes, crayons, brushes, easels and drawing boards. One person had to steer, the other had to shift, and Mrs. Wheeler almost died of fright on the way. Finally we got set up in the window. Now I know how a goldfish feels. All those hundreds of people staring over my shoulder. Although I was all geared up to do or die for the Center, I found my hand was shaking like a leaf. My picture looked like a plea for the Backward Children's Home. Just hope the crowd thought it was modern art.

Did I say ten pages? I really must study for my English final tonight. I absolutely HAVE to get an A for I've been letting my studies slide outrageously largely due to a certain young woman at Downer Sem.

I hope you can come to the lake. Under my strenuous insistence, my mother did write yours, but we have heard nothing yet. When are you going to let me know? Bring a tennis racket; I hear there are new courts in a big field west of the cottage. I asked my father about transportation, and he says there are buses from Milwaukee. From Delavan you can take a cab to our cottage—everyone knows where it is. My father wants me to say he's sorry he can't come to

Milwaukee to pick you up, but he goes back to Des Moines the day
after he drives the family out.

You shouldn't mind that your family never talks. Mine talks all the
time and still nothing gets said. Seriously, shall I write your mother
and ask her why you can't ditch Granny? I bet she'd answer.

Saw "The Red Shoes" last night on your recommendation. Thought
the dancing wonderful, the music discord, the photography stunning,
the acting hammy, the plot childish and all the characters in need of
psychoanalysis.

You should hear me play the "Third Man Theme" and the "Cafe
Mozart Walz." I've rigged up the piano with a few pieces of cardboard
and it sounds just like a zither.

I cannot wait till June. You must come.

Love, Rob

*   *   *

Thursday, June 1, 1950

Dear Rob,

The most terrible thing has happened. Last weekend Sarah Connor, my best friend from Wausau, came down and I took a "weekend." Aunt Marie kindly fixed us up with rooms at a big house on Lake Michigan that's being remodeled for a college dorm—empty except for two women caretakers. Saturday night Connor and I both had dates and had a wonderful evening just acting mad as usual. We said goodbye to the boys at 2 a.m. and toddled off to bed. Slept until 12 the next day when we were awakened by my aunt on the phone ordering us to her apartment in 10 minutes. Connor and I stagger up, dress, and run five blocks without knowing what's happened.

One of the caretakers was there, sneering. "How do you explain your conduct," my aunt hisses, "after I trusted you and went out of my way to accommodate you and your—friend!" "What are you talking about?" says I, paralyzed with surprise and apprehension. Marie glares. "The toilet seats were up!" Connor and I look at each other, wondering whether she's gone mad. Gradually it all comes out. That early morning the good caretaker, passing the bathroom off the front hall, looked in and saw—a raised toilet seat! To Aunt Marie's warped mind only one conclusion presented itself. WE had sneaked MEN into the house and THEY had stayed ALL NIGHT. She called us sluts and is ready to report us to the Downer authorities. She ordered the caretaker to let this go no further as she will take "necessary action."

Needless to say Connor packed her things pronto and sat in the depot downtown three hours until her bus left for Wausau. I was not even allowed to go to the depot, but was sent back to the Sem in disgrace. Connor probably will never speak to me again. And all this for something I didn't do! That night my mother called in tears. "What a ghastly way to treat Marie after all her kindness to you. She will absolutely NOT let you stay at her apartment until you go to Delavan, and in fact, Delavan is out of the question now. How could you!"

I know how Joan of Arc felt at the stake.

So, Rob, I can't come to Delavan. I'm to take the Hiawatha home immediately school is out. Period. I have cried so much that I'm by now resigned—no, never resigned, but in despair. I wanted to come so much.

There won't be a peaceful moment from now till graduation what with exams, baccalaureate, the all-school banquet, awards dinners, graduation practice, shopping for gifts, parties—and I'm wondering how to get through it all. I still haven't told anybody I'm not coming back. I feel dire when Sandy and Robin talk about all the panics we're going to have our big senior year. I haven't told Donald either, or Jack. I go around living a lie.

Your convicted but innocent, Jennie

*　　*　　*

Saturday, June 3, 1950

Jennie, how horrible. You've got to come! I can't believe your mother won't believe your story, even if Aunt Marie won't. It doesn't sound like her at all. And we just got such a sweet note from her, thanking us for the invitation and saying that she knows how much the visit will mean to you. (Mean to you!) It's like a nightmare, and I'm afraid I'm not going to wake up. Please call your mother and try to change her mind. Shall I have my mother write again and tell her how much you're wanted?

Just returned from ushering at Baccalaureate. The senior class was 30 minutes late for the processional. Miss Wolfe kept sending me to the auditorium to inform the concert choir that there would be a slight delay. I'm sure the choir was totally unaware of the fact since they'd been standing at the auditorium door in their hot black robes watching the hands move round the clock for 25 minutes. Finally, however, the graduates arrived, and the choir marched off down the aisle singing "Holy, Holy, Holy." That this was the tune planned for the recessional didn't seem to faze them. It was my responsibility to lead the seniors down to the first row, wait till that row was filled, step back to the next etc.—an impossible job since with all those flowing robes I couldn't see whether a row was filled or not. Consequently all the seniors in the last 10 rows were in the wrong seats. The recessional was vastly better. The choir walked out singing the processional, I motioned the seniors to stand too early with the result that they had to stand staring ahead at nothing for long minutes, the senior line marched out, ragged and unalphabetical, and the ordeal was over.

Have to usher again at Commencement, a very formal affair requiring the ushers to wear dark blue suits. All I own is a conglomeration of plaid sport coats and pants. Either I must break down and buy navy or school traditions will have to bend. I think I know what will happen . . .

Throw yourself on your mother's mercy. Tell her you are expected and that it would be vile manners not to come. Do something. And let me know right away what happens.

Anxiously yours, Rob

*   *   *

Saturday, June 10, 1950

Dear Rob,

I am out of disgrace. Our "crime" has been solved. Two workmen showed up at the dorm on the lake this week and the caretaker let them in. One workman says, "Anybody find a drill press around? I lost it last Friday." Other workman says, "Maybe you left it in the downstairs can." "Can" explored, drill-press found, raised toilet seat explained. But I may never forgive my aunt and I think she owes Connor a written apology.

So I'm coming after all! Right now I'm staying with my aunt but plan to leave the 12th and get into Delavan late in the morning. Then I'll take a cab. The terrible thing is I have to borrow bus and cab money from my aunt, since Elsie sent my allowance to Delavan. What good does it do me there? See you in a mere two days! You'd better be at the cottage to welcome me.

Much love, Jennie

P.S. I'm bringing you a present. Bet you can't guess what.

*   *   *

Monday, June 26, 1950

Dear Rob dear,

How terrible to be back in Wausau again! I feel as though I've been rudely awakened from a wonderful dream. I had—shall I say—a tremendous time. That doesn't express it, but I hope you understand. It seems that each time I see you it gets harder to leave you—oh, I'm determined not to let this letter get all soggy and I won't.

I miss your tousled head and those striped pajamas in the mornings, dodging Muriel constantly, watching the moon rise as we walked along the lake path, but mostly just talking with you. I'm sorry I jumped all over your bed if it made you angry and I'm sorry I kept making you take your glasses off—but you look so sweet without them.

My reception at home was as predicted. Mother: "Honey, what a wonderful time you must have had!" Aunt Marie: "I hope you realize that you have responsibilities this summer. Life is not all play." Grandfather: "Well, well, well, look who's home." Uncle John: "Is this nut brown maiden really Miss McAllister of Downer Seminary?" Grandmother: "Sunburned tramp! I told your mother she was crazy to let you run around the state like a h—r!"

Nine perfect days. Will you ever forget those bridge games when we fixed Muriel's cards and still couldn't win? Getting free rides at the carnival by waving a white handkerchief and muttering "With it!" Dying of laughter at the Tarzan movie surrounded by patrons who obviously did not appreciate your biting wit. Donald constantly on our heels. You know, I'm glad Donald came. I hope he can work out his problems—he's so unhappy now, thinks he's a stupid jerk, so he tries to play big by throwing kids in the lake and smoking three packs a day. But for the first time, I liked him.

Nine almost perfect days. Is it disgustingly selfish of me to wish we'd spent a little more time without Muriel, Carson, Pixie, Roger, and Donald in attendance? And to wish you would hug me and kiss me very hard just once a year? But if you did maybe it would hurt more than it does now to say goodbye.

Don't worry so much about the future, Rob. Just think how many boys go out to face the world with no talent for anything except digging ditches. You have so many possibilities! There's the whole field of art and just about anything in literature and writing. The main thing, I think, is ambition—you've got to be aggressive and persistent to get anywhere, you've got to grab with your teeth onto chances that come along. Now I'm sounding like Aunt Marie. Maybe those books you bought on how to play the stock market will make your fortune!

By the way, Aunt Marie said out of the blue one day that you would make a good professor. I can just see it—mussed old brown suit, glasses on end of nose, books under arm—still desperately playing the stock market and getting poorer every day!

Again, thank you for a wonderful time. Like I told you one night—"You know I love you best." You don't seem to, but I do.

Jennie

RSVP

* * *

Monday, June 26, 1950

Dear Jennie,

I don't really know what to say except that it is very lonely without you. There is no peeling red face to greet me when I pull up the porch shade in the morning, no serious girl to discuss death with, no one to tease (and I really did tease you, though I'm not sure you realized it all the time), no one to drive me crazy by staring into my eyes for hours, no one to toss out of my bed and beat with her own riding crop, no corrupt woman to reform, no one to laugh with, no one to take pictures of, no one to teach me rowdy songs—no Jennie. Indeed, there is now a great void in my life, and though the phrase is trite I mean it seriously. When I think it will probably be a whole year before I see you again, I actually feel ill. Somehow I can't help but feel that we didn't do all the things we should have. I acted so childish much of the time—though it seemed to amuse you. But I wanted so much more.

Did you get to Wausau all right? How is Grandmother? I feel sorry for you back in that house.

Thank you, thank you for the beautiful argyles you left hidden under my pillow. You didn't have to hide them: I wore them today and they look terrific. Of course one is about two inches higher on the leg than the other, but no one will notice. In fact I like them much better this way than if they had been perfect.

Last night I had the dubious pleasure of viewing television for the first time. I hated it. Of course, the show was a rodeo and I detest rodeos and I was also sad about your leaving, but still I will not be broken-hearted if television doesn't come to Iowa.

Roger was just here trying to convince me to see "The Jackie Robinson Story." He failed. I hear the others have decided to go roller skating. I shall stay home. Carson is sitting on my bed right now reading a comic book and discussing his love life. Oh, Jennie.

Today was cloudy and dreary to match my spirits. I kept closing my eyes and seeing your smiling face as you strummed the ukulele and sang "My Foolish Heart."

Will say goodnight now. It's late and I'm weary—as much from thinking about the 365 days that must pass over the face of the earth before we see each other again as from anything. Thanks again for the argyles and for coming out to the lake. I didn't realize how wonderful it was having you here till you left. Such is life.

Love, Rob

* * *

Tuesday, June 27, 1950

Dear Jennie,

Just a note to tell you that we got your gift today. Mother was almost in tears when she opened it. She still hasn't forgiven herself for the way we dropped you in Milwaukee. Please find it in your heart to forgive her. She says to tell you that she's mortally terrified of that side of the family and was worried sick because we were already an hour late. You shouldn't have sent a gift! Maybe Emily Post says you should, but who believes in Emily Post. Just having you here was reward enough.

Muriel has been driving me crazy since you left by bursting into song—and you know what kind of song. I drove Roger, Muriel, and that thug Carson home early last night by playing our song, "Hurry, Hurry, Hurry, Hurry Back to Me" over and over. Will you?

You have left your mark here in more ways than one. Not only do we constantly play "rhythm" on the pier (last night the whole adult population turned out to watch the spectacle), but everybody yells "What a panic!" and Muriel says I've changed. If you were here she would probably whisper "PROGRESS!"

Just came in from swimming across the lake. Since you chose to doubt I could do it, I am having my mother, who paced me in the boat, verify the fact. Time: 50 minutes.

Write often—please. Much love, Rob
Witness: Rob swam across the lake. Annette Faulkner.

*　　*　　*

Monday, July 3, 1950

Dear Jennie,

It is late and most everyone is in bed but I couldn't sleep until I'd got a letter off to you, even though, wretch, the mailbox has been empty the past FIVE DAYS. What have I done to deserve this? Are you belatedly angry at me for stripping all those ID bracelets off your arm and throwing your Pall Malls in the lake?

My parents and Gingy are in Milwaukee and I'm alone. A rare moment. No, my typewriter isn't broken. I'm penning this because you told me you like the personal touch, and even if you can't read my left—handed scrawl I'm going to be personal if it kills me.

Spent the other day in Milwaukee with Donald. We went to Bradford Beach—sacred site—and Donald dropped me temporarily while he pushed girls into the water, untied girls' bathing suit tops, and tackled girls. He knew that in this way he would win many friends of the fairer sex. Walking home from the beach he taught me songs that would make Casanova blush and stole your picture from my wallet. Stole it, remember, no matter what he tells you. I tried to get it back, but Donald is not a halfback for nothing.

That evening Mr. Lindsay drove us downtown to see a stage show. Conversation was limited to questions concerning my family's financial status and club memberships. At the stage show Donald got a huge charge out of several starlets appearing in person (for they were pretty and Donald likes pretty girls) and out of George Jessell's jokes (for they were dirty and Donald likes dirty jokes). I was forced to spend the night at his house where a wild party was in full swing. As a parting gift the next day Donald gave me two books to improve my mind—"Kitty" and "The Passionate Witch." Consider me improved.

If this letter is dirty and crumpled it's because Muriel just bounced in (not everyone was in bed after all) and I shoved it under the cot. Now she has just stamped out, having bitterly informed me, "I know you're writing to Jennie!"

In Milwaukee I went on a spree and bought all "our" music. Your visit has really been stretched. When I get home I can play the songs we sang. You must send the pictures.

We leave here tomorrow. It's going to kill me to leave Wisconsin.

Lots of love, Rob

P.S. How can I end a letter? Love, lots of love, much love—all so overworked, yet how else to send—love.

*   *   *

Saturday, July 8, 1950

Dear Rob,

Forgive me for not writing, but life has been harrowing of late. Last night I had a date and Mother was invited to a party. (Aunt Marie is back in Milwaukee and Uncle John left for Washington.) While my mother was getting ready to go Grandmother grabbed a vase and threw it at the mirror where my mother was putting on lipstick. Well, we both got out fast and went our separate ways. Jim Brandt brought me home about eleven-thirty but I made him say good night at the corner. (He must have thought I was crazy!) I tiptoed up the porch steps and tried the front door. Locked. Side door—locked. Back door—locked.

What a panic, but I was so furious I went round the house banging on doors and windows. Silence. Sat in the garden on a damp bench and smoked two Pall Malls.

About midnight Elsie got dropped off. Needless to say, she was surprised when I emerged from the dark. I suggested yelling and throwing stones at Grandmother's window, but Elsie said, "The neighbors." So we walked downtown to an all-night diner and had coffee to warm our bones. Weird people I've never seen on Wausau streets in daytime! We sat there until 3 a.m. when our money ran out. The rest of the night we spent on the bench smoking cigarettes with our arms around each other to keep warm. Elsie hinted why she's always been afraid to move out, something about a nervous breakdown when she finally did leave home and was found wandering the streets of Milwaukee. Grandmother took the train and brought her back. Ever since, Grandmother's convinced her that if she leaves the house again she will break down.

I told Elsie if we didn't get out I would get out by myself. She cried a little. She doesn't seem to realize I haven't a cent to go anywhere.

Next morning about seven we heard a key turn. Elsie had to get ready to go to work, so we braved it. Grandmother was brewing coffee in the kitchen with her back to us. No one spoke. An hour later Elsie was off to work, but I had nowhere to go. Huddled in my room all day. The phone rang two or three times, I was too afraid to answer. Was it you, Rob? So I'm writing you at last, and when this is finished

I'm going to i-n-c-h downstairs and try to get out the front door to mail it. Can you believe this is me talking? Funny what a night on a bench will do.

I don't know what we'll do, but it can't go on this way, it just can't! The lake is a dream that's fading.

WRITE!

Much love, Jennie

* * *

Friday, July 9, 1950

Dear Jennie,

How terrible. Grandmother sounds insane or intensely warped. Which is it?

Can't write. House is full of relatives and my sixteen-year-old cousin gives me no peace.

Courage. Letter to follow.

Much love, Rob

* * *

Wednesday, July 12, 1950

Dear Rob,

I'm writing this in the breakfast nook of our new apartment! After one absolutely hair-raising fight between Grandmother and Elsie upstairs and down—me finally going after the Witch with her broom, Elsie and I decided we couldn't take it any longer. She took the day off work and we went apartment hunting and found a darling place right across from the Senior High where I'll be going this fall. It's very modern, four rooms, just big enough for two.

Anyway, goodbye to 1016 Washington! Grandmother hates boys, Grandfather, parties, Jews, Catholics, Italians, Polacks—and us. Once she telephoned a Catholic friend of mine and told her I could not associate with a Papist. Is she insane? Whenever her sister Hattie walks down the hill, she shouts obscenities after her from the front porch. Why haven't the neighbors had her committed?

Now at last you can visit me at Wausau! Can you come? There isn't enough room for you to sleep here—the couch is small and sectional—but you could easily stay at the Wausau Club or the Wausau Hotel. Please do come! Will you let me know, though? I'm going to Connor's up north third week in August. Yes, she's still speaking to me. Another house party like last year's and I suppose that again there will be plenty of room under the beds for enterprising young men. Please be one of them.

Donald wrote the other day with vows of undying love and passion. He appears to be taking it hard that I'm not coming back to Downer Sem and as a matter of fact, I'm taking it hard too. He enclosed a sealed envelope containing his predictions as agreed at the lake. I can hear it now: "Rob, you beat my time with Jennie. I should never have introduced her to you. I do not rate because you have beat my time. I hope you will be happy. Your loyal slave to command, Donald McIvor Lindsay. P.S. Rob, you are a dope." I wrote my predictions last week and now we are only waiting for yours. You can trust me to keep them safely till ten years hence when we three shall meet under the same bond of friendship.

The Korean situation looks kind of bad, doesn't it? If war is declared would you have to go? I would die on the spot.

I hear a cat meowing and must go see if we have it for a neighbor. My new address: Same Person, 500 Fulton Street, Same City.
Apartments full of love, Jennie

*   *   *

Tuesday, August 1, 1950

Dear Jennie,

Three cheers and a bottle of rum for you and your mother! Need I say how glad I am that you are in an apartment of your own? Don't feel bad about Downer. Infamous portals! Girls think a hundred times more rot about boys when they're surrounded by females than they do when men are in the picture. Wait and see, you'll be bored with our gender after a while. Of course it may be that I'm just glad you won't be close to Donald. I know the fatal attraction he holds for you.

Am reading Richard Halliburton's books and am aflame with the desire to follow in his footsteps. God, wouldn't it be glorious to go adventuring around Europe and the Americas. I too want to swim the Grand Canal and the pool of the Taj Mahal, I want to fly over the Sahara and climb the Matterhorn. What heaven! Why weren't you a boy? You could join me then. Of course, you could join me anyway, but I'm afraid the management would do some heavy frowning.

Then too Europe is in such a miserable state right now with Russian zones, British zones, and American zones. And everyone sure that World War III is on the way. Guess my galavanting will have to wait. If war is declared I suppose I would have to go—at least I hope so. I really think I'd get rather a charge out of being in the army.

I received a similarly passionate letter from Donald, urging me to get on the stick, telling me I'm a dope, and assuring me he would like to "kiss the hell out of you." Donald's a good kid. Maybe I'll take him on my little sojourn. He's so muscular I know I could find a way for him to do the work for both of us.

Damn and blast Sarah Connor. I have all sorts of invitations to spend days and weeks with friends in various parts of Wisconsin this August. Thought I might get to see you, but you'll probably be in the wilderness entertaining those enterprising young men. Even if I could make it to Wausau, the hotel or Club sound, shall we say, expensive. Don't you have a rescue mission to accommodate one of my means? Why don't you trip down to Milwaukee. Surely a Downer friend could put you up. And then there's Donald's.

Got some of the pictures I took at the lake the other day. Ah, what a beautiful industrious doll you are! Knitting, setting the table, washing windows, wiping plates—not quite the worldly woman Aunt Marie seems to think you are. I'm enclosing the first batch, the second anniversary edition. All in all, I think they're "hangin".

Love, Rob

*   *   *

Thursday, August 10, 1950

Dear Rob,

Leaving tomorrow for Connor's lake house. The dear girl is driving down, picking me up and then we're off for a week of wild times. Think! MEN under the beds. And you could have been one of them.

How I would love to fly over the Sahara and climb the Matterhorn with you. What does it matter I'm not a boy! It's cruel of you to say you'll take Donald just because he has muscles when you know I'm the Ideal Traveling Companion. But the way it looks, there probably won't be any Europe after the Russians and Americans are through fighting it out. Jim Brandt got his notice for joining up. He must report within twelve days when called. It makes me sick. If I were a psychiatrist I'd say you wanted to join the army simply to put off an undecided future. But I'm not.

Elsie and I are slowly adjusting to life out from under The Shadow. Only tragic thing about the apartment is there's no room for a piano unless we move all the furniture out of the living room, to where. I just bought our "Green Cathedral." Makes me wild not to be able to crash into those thrilling chords.

Elsie is horrified you thought you'd have to pay for lodging if you came. She would pay. NATURALLY!

Wausau High, I have found, speaks a very strange language. If you're happy, you have the "glids." If you're sad, you have the "sids." If you have the "greeds" you make out too much on a date. To forward females the boys say, "Keep away" or "Oh yes, mm-hm." Everything good is "salty," everything bad is "nil." A new expression has begun to creep in—"hangin' right in there."

Orson Welles as Harry Lime in "The Third Man" sidled into town the other day and my friend Dodie and I rushed to see him. She made me sit through it twice and when we left I had a huge headache and a huge crush on Orson. Speaking of culture, there is a radio program that dramatizes famous works of literature. FAMOUS, got that? This week it was "Tess of the D'Urbervilles," the book you swore you'd never heard of when we played 20 questions at the lake. And you doubted me.

Must run and mail this. I know you will not live until you get it. Please write me soon (not three weeks, no, please, no). Elsie will forward a letter to Connor's. I'll answer tout de suite.

Needless to say, MY affections do not lose their fervor during the long, hard year.

Jennie

*   *   *

Thursday, September 14, 1950

Dear Jennie,

It's been awhile, hasn't it.

I don't know why I am writing this tonight. By rights I should be in bed as I have to get up at a vile 7:15 tomorrow. I'll have to limit this communication to only the most drastic events in my life.

Definitely the most drastic is the fact I (God save me) am working. Honestly, what a great old job it is—ushering down at Des Moines most glamorous movie palace. The pay is paltry, but there are compensations. I spend relatively little time guiding old ladies to their seats. Most of the time I'm rushing proofs, stills and time charts to the newspaper, giving out passes to Des Moines' privileged, dashing transcriptions over to the radio station, and paying Paramount's bills (I'm very good at this—never seem to get the receipt authorized correctly, and petty cash is disrupted for days). The day after I began they hired a whole string of new ushers so immediately I had four men under me. I love giving orders when I know nothing more than the underlings. The usher immediately my superior is my bosom pal, and the people above him are all good souls. But the job has kept me very busy. Before school started I was at the theatre ten hours a day—we were shorthanded and had two premiers in two weeks.

The last semester of my senior year—God, how awesome. I have a frightful schedule of hard subjects that I didn't want to take. I also have a phantom locker mate whom I haven't seen yet but who wreaks terrible havoc on the contents of my locker. He may hope I never catch up with him.

Don't confuse the issue. I am NOT eager to join the army. I just meant that I wouldn't try to dodge the draft. And you are not a psychiatrist, my dear. My unsure future has nothing to do with it. The outlook for me is not as dismal as you seem to think. It's just that the army would be a cheap way to see the far parts of the globe. Of course they'd probably stick me behind a drawing board doing pretty posters to cheer our doughboys in the mire of Timbuctoo.

How was your vacation at Sarah's? Did you manage to keep your pajamas buttoned? I suppose school is off to a roaring start. How do you like being surrounded by boys again?

I have dozens of other things to tell you, but must end this now—

Write soon.

Much love, Rob

* * *

Monday, September 25, 1950

Dear Rob,

This is going to be a hard letter to write—in fact I feel as though I am writing in a dream. But two letters from you since August 1, two? It has become all too apparent that No. 12 on your list has become too much of a strain to carry on a correspondence with. You told me once that you write the kids at Delevan Lake twice as often as you write me. I didn't say anything, but that broke my heart. In short, I'm so tired of beating my head against a stone wall, waiting for the mailman, pulling out one little letter a month, trying to make someone like me who is 350 miles away.

I've realized (at last, you breathe) that we will never be more than friends. I once wanted more, I was sure you did. But now even friendship seems hard over the miles that separate us. I don't know what's happened, Rob, but something has. I have always prided myself on being your favorite person, but I'm beginning to realize that just because you are mine, the reverse doesn't have to be true.

It seems to me that you are not mature or independent enough to love anybody. Most boys your age—well, that's none of my business. It's just that I'm tired. I used to love you so much (not only romantically) and I'm tired of getting nothing but a monthly letter in return.

So you see, I'm releasing you. You won't have to wonder any more why you're taking the time to write. I've loved knowing you (is it only two years? it seems like ten), but Rob, I'm giving up.

I wish you would answer this. And don't bother to be clever or amusing. I've had enough of that.

Jennie

*   *   *

Tuesday, October 10, 1950

Je vous aime!
Je vous adore!
Quoi d'autre
Voulez-vous encore?

*   *   *

Saturday, October 28, 1950

Since the lines are in French how do I even know you know what they mean?

Actions speak louder than words. One letter a month isn't enough for me, Rob, even though I know you're busy. I can't live on it. I'm busy too, but I could write every week, every day, if you wanted it.

You see, with nothing to go on except an occasional letter and one week together out of the whole year, I find it hard to believe. That's why I wrote you that wonderfully hasty letter saying all the wrong things. I meant that if you were willing to write more often I'd try to be content, but if you aren't—well, why just make me wait? Why let it go on? Why not just end it completely. I don't know, don't know, don't know. You seem to need me very little, Rob. I need you a lot. You probably know.

Jennie

*   *   *

Monday, October 30, 1950

Dear No. 12 (I seem to have forgotten your name),

What silly little ideas you seem to have picked up somewhere. That first letter of yours was a dilly—caused me great concern, so let's get some facts straight right now. You despair of trying to make someone (that's me) like you when you are 350 miles away. Of course, you have every reason to believe I hate you. I always carry on correspondences with people I loathe. I do this so I can rejoice when their letters don't come. And all my arch enemies receive invitations to Des Moines and Delavan so I can detest them at close range.

You also realize that we "will never be anything more than friends." Well, sweetheart, let's see what Webster has to say about the word "friend"—I quote: "One who entertains for another such sentiments of esteem, respect, and affection that he seeks his society and welfare." We also find that a friend can be a "paramour of either sex." (Oh my red face!) I don't know about you, but judging from the above I am perfectly content to be your friend and nothing more.

You also say that friendship seems hard over the miles of lake and land that separate us. Since when are you in a position to say what I find difficult over miles of lake and land! I will admit that I feel a little strange when I see you after an interval of six months, but that just adds to the experience.

Then you feel sorry for yourself too because you only get one letter a month. For the last 30 days I have been leaving home at eight a.m. and not returning till twelve. I only talk to my folks on rare days off and over the phone. There is that wonderful but trying job that keeps me in the theatre one-third of my life. There is school. I am a second-semester senior now and heading for a nervous breakdown. Themes, reports, talks, senior meetings, senior committees. I've been reading two novels for English simultaneously—Dickens and Eliot—and trying to get a huge senior theme out of the way. I've been shopping for colleges and scholarships. Don't forget the piano and art lessons which have been falling by the wayside. My social life has been nil. Not one dance have I been to, not one football game. Managed to squeeze in a Halloween party (came late, left early). I usually slide between the sheets at one a.m. Strange to say, my bleary eyes and muddled head do not feel much like composing sparkling letters at that hour. If you'd like, perhaps I can slip out a postcard per day plus the monthly letter. Would that make you happy?

Dear No. 12, another letter arrived from you today. It was an improvement over the first and I—luckily having the night off—dropped my art work, piano, senior theme, committee ideas, and wrote to you.

I don't know if this will do anything to make you "believe"—but we can hope. You know there are two well-worn sayings that might fit here: "Absence makes the heart grow fonder" or "Out of sight, out of mind." Both can't be true, but I know which one I favor.

> Je vous aime,
> Je vous adore—
> Quoi d'autre
> Voulez-vous encore?

I know what it means, too. Rob

* * *

Thursday, November 2, 1950

Friend, as in Webster's,

I hesitate to write. How do I know you'll be able to snatch a minute from your day to read this?

Things have been plenty busy in Wausau too. Last Friday I answered a knock on the door and opened it to—Donald. In St. John's uniform. Standing there. I almost collapsed—not you understand—from ecstasy. He coolly informed me that he was on "furlough," had stolen his roommate's car, had driven 90 miles an hour from Delafield to Wausau, and that he was ready "to hit the town."

I told him I had to leave in five minutes for work and wouldn't be through until nine. (I too have a job, selling sportswear at a Miljay's Dress Shoppe.) He said he'd be at the curb waiting for the store to close. He was. He had found out (god knows how) that there was a senior dance at the YWCA and insisted we go. I shuddered at the thought, but reasoned that the hall would be dark and that we'd only dance a couple of dances around the edge and tiptoe out. We danced a dozen dances in the middle of the floor and everyone met Donald. In fact, the senior girls, who are bored to tears by high school boys, swarmed him. He was a horrible success. They thought he was just hangin'.

After the dance, six of us piled into the stolen car and drove out to a kind of casino on the Wisconsin River. Just Donald's style: smoky, dark bar, pin-ball machines, gambling in the back room. He insisted we all order lobster tail and paid for everything. On the way home we all sang at the top of our lungs, even Donald who can't sing. Then came the task of getting rid of him for the rest of the weekend. I told him in the most discouraging terms that I had to work from 9 to 4:30 the next day (true), that there was nothing doing Saturday night (false), that he must return his roommate's car before he's arrested (probable). Nothing could dissuade him from staying until late Sunday afternoon. He saw all the sights, met all my friends, did the place up red. The thought that these were the things I'd planned to do with you if you'd come last summer killed me. But no, it had to be Donald.

Yes, busy. Tonight a movie and tomorrow a party for the senior play cast. I'm also on the publicity committee, writing up notices and making posters. Then there's church choir, chemistry (I'm so in the dark), biology (darker), and English which I ace by virtue of pretending to read two times a week.

Now I've sufficiently shown off by giving you a sample of my schedule, I have to dash. You aren't the only one who's busy . . . So—do write.

Love, Jennie

*   *   *

Wednesday, December 6, 1950

Dear Jennie,

One shouldn't begin on a negative note, but may I say I feel low tonight? The reason? Just saw the proofs of my graduation photos.

Nothing more cruel than an unretouched photograph! Gingy had some taken at the same time. They were fresh, sunny; but mine . . .

Received a photo from your Wausau visitor yesterday. When I placed his portrait in my gallery in the place of honor beside yours, I had a startling revelation. Are you sure you and Donald aren't long-lost sister and brother? You have exactly the same dark hair and eyebrows, blue eyes, black eyelashes, and short noses! It's amazing. If you don't believe me, look for yourself.

May I say that I too am not exactly overjoyed at the thought of Donald doing the town with you in Wausau instead of me.

I concede defeat, dear. You are obviously a busy little beaver too. However, I wish I were busy in the same way: parties, dances, plays, movies. I am too busy to be busy, if you know what I mean. It costs me a small fortune to go anywhere, since I have to pay someone to work for me at the theatre. Just taking my distant cousin Cindy (visiting again) to a drive-in movie cost me $7 for the evening. Then too the whole staff at ye olde Paramount fell ill except yours truly. I put in twelve hours overtime last week. Just think of all the words I could have written to you instead.

Have finally laid eyes on a copy of "Tess of the D'Urbervilles." Good old Dorothy Jenkins (you remember good old Dorothy?) is reading it. Just finished "The Mayor of Casterbridge" for Brady. Very sad—cleft my heart in twain. Tess one day in the near future, but first must polish off Woolf, Faulkner, and Millay.

My life has become schizophrenic. There's school with boring classes, boring meetings, and boring students. Then there's the Paramount, a wildly different, dark world. Most kids who work there are dropouts, some are on drugs, and Dolores, the pale blonde behind the candy counter, plies another trade after the theatre closes. The Paramount bunch are all misfits in one way or another. I leave you to guess which world I prefer.

Do you have any plans after graduation? I'm still in the dark. Terrible, isn't it—not knowing what's to become of one a month and a half from now.

I'll hurry this to a close for I know you are too busy to spend much time poring over lengthy messages. Will be hearing from you soon, I trust.

Your ever lovin' friend, Rob

* * *

Saturday, January 6, 1951

Dear Rob,

Your post card inspires me to write you a lengthy epistle. I'm sorry you didn't call New Year's Eve. You wouldn't have wakened anyone. I got in at 3 a.m. and Elsie at 5!

Thank you for your senior class picture. It's sweet and sulky, and then those neat brown eyes! I'm going to pick up my senior pictures soon. If you like short curly hair, long curly eyelashes, a shiny nose and a fakey smile, you'll love it.

Christmas vacation has gone like the wind. I hate to think of school Monday. There were eighteen parties—formals, toboggan parties, tea—dances, etc. I've ruined my love life in Wausau for the rest of the year. You see, the senior boys deeply complain that the senior girls go out with them during school year, but that the minute the college boys come home we cut the seniors out for all formal dances and holiday parties. I swore to Jim Brandt (a senior I date sometimes) that I was different. For one thing, having been at Downer, I don't know any college men. Then the first night of Christmas vacation I met a college man and whirled off my feet, went out with him every night. Paul Krueger, however, left for Madison before school started. Next night there was a girl-ask-boy party. I asked Jim. He accepted but was bitter, bitter. Do you have problems like that in your school?

How has it been with you? I got a pair of skis for Christmas and have ventured up Rib Mountain even though downhill terrifies me. My friend Jane goes with me, but she's honest. She just poses in front of the fireplace in a smashing ski outfit smoking Viceroys. Hearing from Donald regularly, Jim Gordon de temps en temps.

Please, mon vrai vrai ami, send something besides postcards.

Love,
Jennie

*   *   *

Thursday, January 11, 1951

Dear Jennie,

Six more days and I'll no longer be a high school student. Believe me, I won't miss it since I plan to go right to college—that is, if I get a scholarship. If not, no college until I do—my lawyer dad refuses to underwrite a career in art. Can't see how I'll ever rate—have been letting my studies slide tragically. Don't have anything to show for a whole semester of pot throwing in Art. Miss Wheeler has been giving me A's for rosy memories of past accomplishments, but when she finds out how little clay and I agree it'll be curtains. I have to be in the top 15% of the class to get a scholarship, and though my classmates are 99% cretins, I'm going to have to hit the books.

After a period of comparative disinterest, Gloria has redoubled her efforts to capture me. Why don't you rescue me? We could go to the prom—that is, we could go to the prom if I were going, but I made a rather impassioned public announcement that I wouldn't be seen there if they paid me. I cannot be reconciled to the prom committee's inane way of handling the affair.

SKIING, please write of it no more. How I long to go skiing again. But Des Moines is depressingly flat and besides I don't have time. Sun Valley must be heaven—or Hawaii or Tahiti for that matter. The grass is always greener, you know: but how can I tell unless I go to Cairo and Cathay, whether this blessed spot I know is blessed in every way. That's incorrect Millay, but you get the gist. Oh well, at least I have the rolling hills of Korea to look forward to. Know I'll hate the army if and when . . . regimentation, Boy Scouts senior grade.

At the Paramount I'm a wheel now and give more orders than I take. Besides I like meeting the public, both good souls and the heels. You'd be surprised how much you can tell about a person just by the way he asks where to find the restroom. I'm also becoming an expert on sex fiends. You'd be more than surprised how many people come to the movies not to see the show. Have many a tale when next we meet.

Well, baby dear, try to find a little time between those entangled love affairs to scratch out a little letter for me. And please send your class picture—curly hair, curly eyelashes and all.

Love, Rob

*   *   *

Monday, February 12, 1951

Dear Rob,

Life is peculiar. I don't know why, but it seems of late that I have been throwing aside all the things that mean so much to me in favor of some new wild life. One fine calm day, my old life will come back to me. Until then I feel like a puppet jerked about by a frantic demon of fun.

I believe I told you about Paul Krueger? The college man? I guess it's understood that I'm "going with him." Je ne sais pas. He's a brain. Straight A's through nursery, grade, Sunday, and high schools. Currently third in his class at the University of Wisconsin. Student council president, WHS, DAR, Badger State, Sigma Chi ad nauseum. I go with him partly for mercenary reasons. He is a chemistry genius and right now I'm in a total fog over equations. When he's home or lends me his old chemistry workbook I magically get straight A's. Besides, ever since Mr. Johnson, the chemistry teacher, discovered I'm "going with" his ex-prize pupil, he's been falling over his feet to give me extra help. I need it. Paul is going to be a surgeon, therefore he has been deferred from service for four years. He has blond hair, black eyebrows, and blue eyes. He comes from a wealth-ridden family.

We're moving. The landlord raised the rent New Year's Day, and Elsie can't afford ninety dollars a month. Our new address will be 511 Franklin Street. I don't know how we're going to survive in one room plus tiny kitchen and bath, though it's a big room with a fireplace. Maybe I can get a piano.

I love Millay—

> I cannot tell how many loves
> Have come and gone.
> I only know that summer
> Sang in me a little while
> That sings no more.

Shortly after Christmas I sprained my knee skiing because I really can't ski. A month later, Jane and I drove into the country to look at an old farm we dream about buying and fixing up. Car went into snowy ditch and in the process of trying to heave it out I sprained the other knee. That too healed. Yesterday in gym class an over—enthusiastic guard managed to trip me and I now have a sprained ankle. I shall become a book worm.

Do you like Perry Como's "If"? He's usually too mushy for me, but I'm mad, simply MAD about it.

Meeting Elsie in a minute to pick out new curtains for the new apartment.

Write soon.

Much love, Jennie

*　*　*

Saturday, February 17, 1951

Darlin',

Isn't it grand! We're both so happy. Don't ask me why, but I have been absolutely delirious these last few weeks. God knows, I've never had so much to do, but I've never had so much fun doing it either. I know exactly how you feel—I feel like I'm being absolutely driven, but it's a glorious ride. With you it seems to be love or a reasonable facsimile, don't know what it is with me.

Drake is a joy! Much easier than high school. I got two scholarships (one for being an artist, one for being a brain), so it's not costing much. I love all the kids. They're so much brighter and more original than the high school crowd. My art classes are near riots. Though I imagined antiquated professors in long black robes and flowing beards, the faculty aren't much older than the students. The freedom is wonderful. No more worries about being late or absent.

I'm reading to a blind student. It's like being paid for doing homework—we have the same classes and I would have to read the assignments anyway.

Things at the Paramount are also better than ever. Someone discovered I could type, so now I spend 9/10 of my time in the central office pounding out payroll checks, comparative reports, show schedules, usher schedules and bank night forms. For some insane reason, these all have to be done in quadruplet or octetlet. I am spreading the word that if I were managing Tri-State Theatres I'd cut needless reports and save a million a year.

Gym is the only thorn in my side. I have always loathed all sports except skiing, skating and swimming. Drake has no pool so I must take gym. I don't know who's most to be pitied—my instructor, my fellow gymnasts, or me. It all started the day the instructor announced we would start with basketball. All the little sportsmen cheered. I groaned. Haven't played the game since 8th grade. Oh, it's hell, I tell you, absolute hell. My team has yet to win a game and it's all my fault. Thank god it's only a forty minute class.

My birthday was distinguished by Gloria calling long distance to wish me bon day, a card from Muriel, and a card from Donald announcing he has a new love. Georgia something. He sounds quite serious. Would that Gloria find a new love. Even the miles can't keep her off my neck: I've been swamped with letters. Muriel, incidentally, enclosed a picture. Remember at the lake how she cried when Mason told her she couldn't come for a ride because she'd sink the boat? No more pudge. What a change. She must have lost forty pounds. She says she hardly eats because she doesn't like food any more. I don't know if that's good or bad, but it's paid off. She looks like a pin-up girl.

I thought you were the woman who adores dark men. James Mason, Tyrone Power, remember? Who said a blond would get you in the end—one of those crazy fortune-telling crones you patronize? I too could be a blond with black eyebrows. After reading your letter I dashed out for peroxide and am almost ready to pour it on. Of course you can't describe the Falkners as wealth-ridden. Pity.

Did you see "Johnny Belinda"? There's a deaf mute like the girl Jane Wyman plays in my creative design class, and my heart absolutely goes out to her, for the class is such a talk-fest that she is just OUT. What's more she is about the most beautiful thing I have ever seen. If it were not for her handicap she would be the most popular girl in the school. I have nightmares about it.

You never deserved such a long or prompt letter. WOULD YOU PLEASE BE KIND ENOUGH TO SEND ME YOUR SENIOR CLASS PICTURE? There, I have asked and will not ask again, for I too am tired of beating my head against a stone wall.

Much love, Rob

*　　*　　*

Tuesday, February 27, 1951

Dear Rob,

I was unreasonably glad to get your letter. So prompt and six pages. As soon as I'm finished with this I'll mail my picture. Heaven forbid there should be any stone walls for you.

Donald writes weekly about his progress with Georgia. I am so keenly interested. His last letter reminisced: "I was a dog at the lake last summer. I could have kicked myself to pieces after I left. You and Rob are my two best friends and I treated you like dirt." Poor Donald—and I thought he behaved very well. He wants us to have a big THIRD reunion this summer and promises he'll behave. We must have it with hot dogs on Bradford Beach.

Congratulations on your scholarships! I wasn't aware that you're at Drake University. Shows how well you keep me informed.

I tagged along to Madison with the debate team last weekend and managed to see Paul some of the time. Told the debate coach I absolutely had to see the state capitol for historical reasons, slipped his custody and joined Paul at the Rathskeller. Dark walls, old benches and tables, beer steins. Paul ist zehr German, taking the language, and is trying to teach me basics. I can now say "Tanz mit mir," "Guten Nacht, mein Lieb," "Wir werden ein gute Zeit haben" and "Mit viele liebe." Fluent, eh? But like a German, Paul is intolerant. He writes me paragraphs of German which I must painstakingly translate or live in fear he does not love me. Yet he is outraged when I toss in a French phrase for him to bite on. I've decided that brilliant people do not care to have others demonstrate their own tiny accomplishments.

You said you know exactly how I feel, how gloriously, deliriously happy I am. I'm sure you know nothing about how I feel. Nothing at all, nothing at all.

Please, after reading to your blind friend, find time to write to your other blind friend, blind because all who love are . . .
Jennie

*   *   *

Thursday, April 27, 1951

Dear Jennie,

At last spring has come to Iowa. After three weeks of rain, snow, and frigid cold, the sun has decided to shine and the hyacinths to bloom.

I suppose you are slightly irritated by the slowness of this letter, but I'm not going to try to explain because it would be the same old story. And you would reply, "If you don't have time to write me you must hate me." And I would have to assure you I don't and write six letters a week for a month to make it up to you. After all, does one letter a month—or even one letter every two months—mean a person likes a person less than four letters a month? I don't think so . . .

We really MUST have a reunion on Bradford Beach this summer. We haven't been there, all three of us, since that first summer three years ago.

Drake is becoming rather trying. Our soc professor pulled a filthy trick this morning by switching test questions, and we who had been furnished with advance information were rather put out. I probably passed with flying colors anyway, but it was a shock to learn that the old prof is wise to us. Frankly, I'm relieved: my faith has been renewed. Madness to complain, but college simply is not challenging enough. I can sleep in class, avoid all my assignments, and still get an A. Never mind—I'm devoting my time to the stock market instead.

Thank you for the picture. It graces my room and I tinted it beautifully (did you know I have a job tinting portraits?). You look fresh and shining and so typically American high school girl. Only I wish you would let your hair grow. Just a little? Two inches? One? Just for me? You can always cut it off again, you know.

Ahhh, the radio just gave out with "How High the Moon." My favorite. I think the ending is ecstasy. I am also having a passionate love affair with Rachmaninoff's Second Piano Concerto, bought the music, and am slowly memorizing its fifteen pages. It's a bit sketchy without an 80 piece orchestra behind me, but I manage to rise above that.

Be hearing from you soon? (Hopefully, pleadingly, and humbly I ask.)

Mit viele liebe, Rob

* * *

Monday, May 1, 1951

Dear Rob,

You don't know how glad I was to find something in the mailbox besides a scrawl from Donald and an overdue library notice. You know, though—somewhere along the line you have twisted my complaint. I don't think that when you don't write you hate me. I only think you're indifferent, and indifference to me is worse than hate. Does one letter a month, you ask, mean a person likes a person less than four letters a month? Yes, it does. But you don't think so, and you're writing the letters.

Life is dull right now—lack of homework, spring inertia, breaking up with Paul, no job, school droning on and on, yet no idea what to do after graduation.

The only lively moment in the abyss of abyssmalness was the prom last Friday night. The evening began spiritedly with a cocktail party, then the dance. (Remember how I used to tell you all about what I wore? Can't resist. Floating pink chiffon skirt with a pink strapless satin top sparkled with rhinestones. I charged it at Miljay's, I am their slave for life.) Afterwards we went to The Palms, a rather swank place for Wausau, and waited three and a half hours to be served. Jane and I, bored to tears, played the slots in the back room. At 3:30, just as our waitress came round the corner loaded down with our orders, we stalked out of the place. We did not deign to return. One of the lads said he knew a great place to eat in Antigo, so four cars trailed his forty miles through the night. Great spot closed. At 5 we landed at a greasy spoon called "Need a Feed" near Merrill. Not that feed we didn't. Six a.m. back in Wausau atop Rib Mountain, squatting over a smudge that stubbornly refused to roast our hot dogs. Through the mist the sun rose looking like an overdone fried egg. Would have welcomed one. Drove back into town about seven. Fell asleep in Bill Armstrong's car, was rudely awakened when his father came to claim it. Staggered down the block to another all-night promer's house, burned waffles, fell asleep on all six beds.

Please, could you manage to write me before summer? Do you want to see me?

My favorite song is "How High the Moon" too.
Thank you again for writing.

Love, Jennie

*   *   *

Saturday, May 5, 1951

Dear Jennie,

Thank you for your quick and amusing reply. It took me hours to get up enough nerve to open the envelope. It came so promptly that I expected the worst.

You sound bored with it all. How well I understand. Now that the novelty has worn off, college has settled down to pretty much of a grind. Classes are tedious, reading to Bob is a chore, gym is unbearable. I don't know, but college is not what I expected—not the "challenge" my high-school advisors so vividly advertized. Most students are fawning simpletons and I'm disillusioned. Maybe I've been reading too much Dreiser and Sinclair Lewis.

Work at the Paramount has also become a drag. When I started, ushering was a novelty, now it's tedious. The candy stand was new, now it's too familiar. Office work was fun, now it too is stale. The sex maniacs were interesting, now they're just pathetic. If not for the free movie passes I believe I would quit.

Sometimes you ask the most brainless questions. Of course I want to see you this summer. I cannot imagine a summer in which I would not want to see you. Would you like to come to Delavan again? God, it will be nice just to lie on a pier with nothing to think about and nothing to do after this insane dashing from pillar to post that my life has been this year. When are you sprung from school?

If you can dig it up in some obscure book of essays, Max Beerbohm's "How Shall I Word It?" is highly hilarious—the one worthy piece in our English text and of course the only one we have not been required to read.

But enough! I hear a horn. Friends outside. They expect to find me ready and waiting. What fools they be!

Love, Rob

*   *   *

Saturday, July 2, 1951

Dear Rob,

I've just splashed my way home through puddles, plueve, and parapluies. Wausau is having its great annual rainy season. Since it's a strain to peer at the outdoor movie through streaming windows, I wish it would stop.

Thank you for making this summer in Milwaukee another one of those wonderful times I always have when I am with you. I'm so glad you could stay three whole days at Marietta House. I wish it had been longer, but I felt you did enjoy being with me.

The night after you left Donald took me to a carnival. The Loopo plane got stuck in flight and naturally I got sick. To cheer me, Donald tried the shooting gallery and actually won me an enormous white teddy bear with a yellow bow. I've never won a teddy bear—never known anyone who has—just seen seedy looking strangers walking away with them tucked their arms. Donald was civilized and attentive, he was more than civilized and attentive—he was kind. I'm afraid Georgia may be out of the picture and Jennie back in.

I think this was the nicest time the three of us have had. No serious battles, no little cruelties like eluding Donald or laughing behind his back. When my cab left for the train, Donald reached under his raincoat, took out a gardenia corsage in a box, and handed it to me saying solemnly "Moon, moon, clair de lune"—our "poem," remember? I went into hysterics and the three other occupants of the taxi eyed me askance all the way to the station.

Moon moon claire de lune. I will marry Donald.

Please do write soon.

Love, no not one love, but hundreds of them—Jennie

*   *   *

Tuesday, July 10, 1951

Dear Jennie,

You should talk about rotten weather. Since I've been back in Iowa we've had two sunny days. Naturally I had to work all afternoon in the dark caverns of Paramount on both of them. I have become a denizen of darkness, ambling in the shadows, playing in the night. My tan has faded, my tennis muscles gone slack. My cousin Cindy, who was visiting, had to take off in a thundrous downpour. To make it worse, she was the only passenger on the plane. It's raining at this very moment. Should I start knocking together an ark?

I'm enclosing prints of the scads of pictures we took in Milwaukee. Don't know what happened—so many seem to be shrouded in mist. Anyway it was fun—never willI forget that Sunday drive when you decided in the middle of a teeming intersection that you couldn't drive and dove into the back seat. Or that frigid Saturday picnic minus the food.

Have returned to my job—under protest. They lured me back to Paramount with talk of a raise and promotion. Before I knew it I was back at the typewriter five hours at a stretch, pounding out payroll checks, fund reports, box office reports, schedules. Then I had to stamp and give out 1700 passes to last night's midnight show crowd as a promotional gimmick. Naturally only seventy people showed up, so all the ushers went home with 200 stamped passes crammed in their pockets to distribute to sons and lovers. How many would you like?

Got to eat and run—

Much love, Rob

*   *   *

Saturday, July 21, 1951

Dear Rob,

Thank you for your letter and the absolutely dreadful snapshots. I'm back at work at Miljay's Dress Shoppe, trying to convince "madam" that she looks devastating in this top or that golf skirt when actually she looks a fright. Today one of my Downer dearest dropped in—Sandy Erwin, co-respondent in many crimes. I fell upon her with cries of joy. At the same time I was terribly embarrassed to be found working. Isn't that insane? I'm sure she didn't think a thing of it, though she's probably never worked a day in her life.

Asking her for news of St. John's, I discovered she's been dating my old flame, Jack Rees . . .

I have been dating a third year medical student named Sheldon, and although he's a fine lad I always feel nervously naked under his eye—sure he's absorbed in my bone structure or something worse. One night however (he is something like you—I am lucky—one finds so few intelligentia humanus) he quoted some really lovely poetry to me. All I can recall are two lines:

Come away, come away death,
And in sad cypress let me be laid . . .

After saying "sad cypress" over and over, I feel quite resigned to dying. Try it.

Another night in different mood, this medical student and I decided to observe the other half at the Waupaca Chain o' Lakes Casino, a place famous for big-name bands and rowdiness. You would have loved it, Rob—all the bleached babes hanging at the bar, begging free drinks. You would have whipped out your drawing pad immediately. The Chain o' Lakes begins at the casino, so we got into bathing suits and plunged in. A couple were paddling a canoe ahead, and we trailed it stealthily down the moonlight until we caught up with it. Mad medical student decides to dive under the craft. Bleached blonde waves her paddle wildly. "Whales!" she screams. Her companion: "Aw, it's only an octopus swimming on the surface!"

I keep thinking about that song you sang when we were walking the beach—"For I was born to wander and I was born to roam." How I wish I could say it about myself, it sounds so free. I'm afraid I wasn't born to wander anywhere. I'll probably have a dozen kids and roam no further than the kitchen sink.

Please do remember me and our good times in Milwaukee and be inspired to write.

Love, Jennie

*   *   *

Tuesday, October 3, 1951

Dear Rob,

What a catastrophe. Your August and September letters seem to have gotten lost in the mails, but not one word of complaint do I offer. After all, does one letter every month—or even one letter every year—mean that a person likes a person less, etc. etc.

I am now a co-ed now at our local branch of the University of Wisconsin. It's fun—so different from high school. I go to Political Science, rush out for a cigarette, go to English, rush out for a cigarette, go to French and stroll home at 11:00. Then having partaken of the nothings in our refrigerator, I saunter back at 2:00 for either History or Botany. If Botany, we go on field trips to Marathon Park and loll on benches while our little gray-tufted German professor tries to pound the "foondimentals" of pinately and palmately veined leaves into our smoke-dimmed brains. For old time's sake look at the back of the last page: you'll find the old rogue's gallery of teachers.

Even though I'm now a co-ed I have not entirely grown up. Scanning the paper one day, I was enthralled to find that a James Mason picture was coming to the Grand Theatre. At ten to seven I was installed in row 2, three fingernails already gone. The opening scene shows a helicopter landing at a lighthouse. Out leaps Mason. I whimper in ecstasy. "I am going to fly in China," announces Mason. "No, no," wails the light housekeeper. "YES!" shouts Mason, dashing to the edge of the rocks and lifting his head to the turbulent heavens, "I AM GOING TO FLY IN CHINA!" Shot of helicopter roaring off into distance. Eagerly I await his return. He cometh not. Not once in the rest of the whole goddamn picture does he cometh. The box office refused to return my money.

Do you remember that stone wall I was always beating my head against? I won't blame you if you don't—those days seem so distant. Sometimes I think it's a shame I stopped trying (I did, you know). Sometimes I think about trying again, but not seriously because I realize the impossibility. But one small, impersonal question. Who is she, Rob, that you can ignore me this way?

Jennie

* * *

Saturday, October 20, 1951

Dear Jennie,

Where to start? So much has happened the last month or two. Might as well begin with last night. Candy girls, cashiers, ushers, and assorted friends went out after the late show and raised general hell. In the course of the evening we were shot at, thrown out of a restaurant, thrown out of a drive-in, and four hours later, after we had dropped off the girls and were driving home, tired and considerably subdued, got pinched for driving forty in a 25-mile zone. What an anti-climax to an evening of mayhem.

Your local institution of higher learning sounds a lot like dear old Drake—even the drawings of your teachers look devastatingly familiar. Think I'll give you a look at some of mine at the end of this letter, as you say, just for old time's sake.

Walked into ROTC class this morning to be confronted by huge red posters screaming WE WANT YOUR BLOOD! I turned green, quivered, and was beating a hasty retreat when jolly old Sergeant Doyle bounded in, locked the doors, and cheerfully announced that the military had decided to see which ROTC unit could bleed the most for the boys in Korea. I told him that since I'd caught pneumonia drilling in sub—zero weather, I needed every drop for myself, but, leering like a vampire, he informed me that glory, country, and honor called.

I was innocently standing on the street corner this afternoon awaiting a bus, when a little old lady with beady eyes, faded fox fur and a bag of celery came up to me. "We have meetings every Saturday night at nine," she hissed in my face. "How fascinating," said I. "You SHOULD come," she replied with much blowing of bad breath my way. I vainly searched the horizon for my bus, muttering that I would think about it. As she faded away into a nearby shadow, she left me with this advice: "Go to the church at Ninth and Pleasant. Harley Smith is going to play hymns on his organ." Do I look like I need saving or diversion—either musical or perverse? Maybe so.

Finally, a few words about that nasty stone wall that keeps cropping up between us. The child with the curly hair just about breaks it down in the summer, but then she goes away . . . and one can do so much rebuilding in 360 days. Every time I see you, it's like seeing you for the first time. Yes, we write letters, but you have to admit these poor pieces of paper are hardly a substitute for the flesh and blood article. Do you understand?

Write soon.

Much love, Rob

*   *   *

Wednesday, November 7, 1951

Dear Rob,

It is 2:00 a.m. and since I'm practically blind from trying to memorize my history text and typing frantically at my newspaper article (I'm the "college correspondent" for the Wausau Daily Record Herald), I've decided to complete the process by writing to you.

More proof that I'm nearly blind is that I had to use Grandmother's golden periscope to see the Wisconsin-Indiana homecoming game. At game time it was 2 degrees above zero and snowing buckets. We passed Rhine wine during the second half to keep bloodstreams flowing. The third time the bottle was passed it didn't come back. We waited fifteen minutes. Then I banged medical student over the head with my pom-pom, the bottle fell from his hand as he was rendered unconscious, and the Rhine flowed again. After three fraternity parties to which M.S. escorted me (or did I escort him?—what do you call it when two lovers—lovers did I say—hold each other up all evening?) we crawled back to the Alpha Phi house on hands and knees through the snow. I left medical student on the front steps. Morning he was still there, so I hauled him into the kitchen and made him eggs. He said, "You don't fry eggs like my mother," so I threw them at him. Grandmother's golden periscope followed. Man's washed up with me. How can I love a fellow who hogs Rhine wine, falls insensible on my doorstep, doesn't flicker when I blow "Good night, sweet prince" into his earmuff, critiques my eggs, and collapses at the mere blow of a golden periscope?

You would not complain about eggs, Rob, would you? Your thoughts are so far above earthly considerations that you would tuck them away in blissful unconsciousness. Wouldn't we make a LOVABLE pair? This is a proposal, I want you to know.

Which brings me to two questions: why don't I build any walls? And why, instead of building yours back up, don't you just let it alone until the next time we see each other? No—I don't understand.

Another question: why am I always making such passionate love to you? Is it because you never make passionate love to me? Would I run if you did? You must know. Someone has to.

Anticipating your answer, I remain (how odd)

Jennie

*   *   *

Sunday, November 11, 1951

Lover,

Proposal accepted! Where shall we go for the honeymoon? That is bound to be a problem for I am torn between Switzerland, Tahiti, and Sun Valley. Saw a movie of skiing in the Swiss Alps, nearly drew all my money out of the bank and flew over. Saw another movie of surfing in Tahiti, and Switzerland lost all its charm. Now have seen a short on skiing and swimming in Sun Valley. Please, though, don't fry me eggs for breakfast. I'm not as far above earthly considerations as you think. Even without a hangover I can't help thinking very earthy thoughts about those yellow yolks being undeveloped chickens.

Speaking of food, I suddenly decided last week that I would look better twenty pounds heavier, so I have leapt into a mad fattening-up process. I eat five meals and thirty snacks a day, consume barrels of apples, drink gallons of milk, and butter my bread three inches thick. Someone told me nervous tension makes one lean, so I no longer worry. I walk instead of run for busses, avoid all homework, skip the weekly dance, forgo movies, and go to bed to read at nine o'clock.

The other night I did relent, and instead of crawling between the sheets after dinner, left the house at midnight to meet the whole Paramount crowd for a weiner roast. Don't know why—guess someone told me that weiners and beer were fattening. We drove out to a deserted spot eight miles from town, sinister even in daylight, and parked the cars. We hoisted firewood and food on our backs (except for the candy girl, who was wearing spike heels), and beat the underbrush in search of a suitable spot. After breaking through ice while crossing a stream, losing three members when a straying horse decided to charge, and nearly falling over an unexpected hundred foot drop, we settled down on frozen ground and had our party. I had been entrusted with the potato chips, and not till I thrust my hand into the bag did I discover that somewhere along the route the bottom had torn off and the chips scattered to the seven winds. Warm beer and burnt weiners proved unfilling, the marijuana passed around contained no calories, and I probably lost five pounds on that little adventure.

Nine o'clock! Curfew is ringing, so alas we must part. Hope you regain your sight. Think what you're missing—sunsets on wintry eves, technicolor movies, and next summer, big brawny me (that will be worth seeing). Then again, this officer training may wear me to a shadow after all. I often wonder which is worse—shooting in Korea or drilling in ROTC—devil take it.

As ever, love, Rob

*   *   *

Friday, November 30, 1951

Dear Fat One,

Set down the beer bottle and banana cream pie and answer me this: wouldn't it have been altogether more considerate to have asked me where I might like to honeymoon? Let me tell you. Paris. London. Venice. Rome.

You know, of course, that Donald now graces the freshman class at the University of Florida. I receive scrawls depicting him lounging at pool's edge surrounded by blondes and plucking oranges while glancing at his toughest textbook, "The Art of Diving." How long do you think he'll last? I can't imagine him in a classroom.

Romance, romance everywhere. Jane, Dodie and I went bowling last eve and I was astonished to find a note from the pinboy in my returned ball—"Will you go out with me after the game? Curly." He ruined my score—could only use two fingers because I had to keep sending him answers. Kept trying to discover what Curly might look like down at the end of the alley behind that mysterious wire screen. Saw him later. Pimples, straight red hair. Awfully glad my ninth-frame note said no.

Went to Stevens Point for a college formal dance last weekend. Had ten whiskey sours, ripped my formal getting it out of the teeth of a black dog, got locked in a private club for two hours, and awoke the dead playing an out-of-tune pipe organ at midnight. Your average weekend.

I also danced with—you'll never guess—Mrs. Van Wagenan's ex—husband. Haven't the foggiest what he was doing there, unless he's on the faculty, nor do I exactly remember how we ended up on the dance floor. He's tall and very thin with hair so blond it's white—not at all the type I'd associate with Mrs. Van. When I said I'd gone to Downer, he said, "Then you must know my ex-wife, Margaret." "Oh, yes, she's the most popular teacher at the Sem." "She would be," he said, "at a girls' school." The band stopped and our dance was over.

Just received news that Richard, one of my loves ("I cannot tell how many, etc.") has gotten his army notice and has to leave the 26th of December. Merry Christmas from the War Department. The whole damn mess makes me sick. Does ROTC defer you from military service? RSVP. I'm confused about this. I should die if you were sent to Korea. Impossible to consider.

Right now I'm existing in that delicious interval between the last class of the day and going to work at Winkleman's, the toy department, no less. Decided that if I wanted to get Elsie something more than handkerchiefs in a cellophane box I'd better get to work. And so she did.

Much love, Jennie

*   *   *

Tuesday, January 1, 1952

Dear Jennie,

First day of the new year, and my first—to you. December has come and gone. What hell it was. Found out at the beginning of the month that my mother had to be operated on for a breast tumor. You know my mother. She gets hysterical if Gingy is half an hour late home from a date or if I leave the house without a scarf. But in a real crisis she is a rock while my dad falls to pieces. The tumor was cancerous, but they think they caught it in time. She was in the hospital over Christmas and just got home two days ago. Need I say that she is keeping up our spirits about the whole ghastly thing.

Then my dad collapsed while giving blood and was rushed to the hospital. Gingy and I were scared to death until it was diagnosed as a rather simple case of overwork and anxiety about Mother. While Dad was in hospital I smashed up the car so that we were without transportation for five days. Gingy and I have been keeping house and it is no fun—almost enough to make me decide not to be a bachelor after all. Got round to opening the Christmas presents yesterday. Very dreary, but then Christmas is these days. College resumes tomorrow at eight a.m.—heaven help me.

The only good thing about December was the news that because of frigid temperatures, ROTC drills would be discontinued until spring. Immediately after the bulletin was issued, the sun came out, temperatures climbed into the sixties, and the Major could be seen out on the deserted drill field tearing out his hair strand by strand.

Not having drill is my one advantage over Donald—he spends his time "picking up babes," "guzzling booze" and "loafing on the beaches"—but in Florida he has ROTC drill all year round. Cannot imagine him in a classroom—except playing with himself in the back row.

Happy leap year. Lost my newly gained twenty pounds welcoming it in at the Paramount. Had to work till one last night. What a mess. We had a Martin and Lewis comedy (they are immensely popular, I cannot say why) and handling the jam proved hell on nerves and muscles: dozens had to be physically restrained from bursting lock-out ropes, attacking candy girls, and boozing during the picture. We did make tons of money, however. It came in so fast we had to stuff it in waste paper baskets. Afterwards the whole staff went out for a celebration, Dolores, our candy counter woman of the night, propositioned me, and everyone got tight on Philadelphia whiskey and rancid gin. The morning papers beat us home and it was a sorry looking bunch that staggered into the theatre this afternoon to work the matinee.

Darling, I would really rather not go to Paris. It has such limited appeal: Follies Bergere, Eiffel Tower, Beaux Arts Ball. Tahiti is much more to my liking. Or South America? Let's sail as deckhands, shall we? So romantic—in the Halliburtonian sense of the word.

May I say it is so like you not to know what Mrs. Van Wagenan's ex—husband was doing at a Stevens Point dance. It would have been my first question. Must leave you for the dark caverns of the Paramount. Yes, they are shorthanded and Rob the Valiant volunteered.

Much love.

* * *

Wednesday, January 9, 1952

Dear Rob,

What a wretched December. I pray your mother will be all right. What a harrowing time for everyone. Now I feel guilty for cursing that month and a half without a letter. I'm sending your mother a tiny gift to cheer me up.

I am writing from a sick bed. Seems I had a bad cold two Thursdays ago. I survived through the following Tuesday night, collapsed on Wednesday, pulled myself together to go out Thursday and Friday nights, and was carried in Saturday morning with the milkman. Pneumonia and a week in bed.

Two proposals over the vacation. Oh, to be strictly accurate, one and a half. Somewhat of a temptation, what with friends popping off right and left with diamonds, but I said no. One chap graduates from Wisconsin this month with a chemical engineering job waiting for him. The other intends to be a corporation lawyer in two years. Both offer shining security. Both frowned when I mentioned my career. Both are faintly boring. Go through life bored?—Nevah!

Thank you, thank you for the picture of you in uniform. Gazing at it I often feel quite sad. My illness, no doubt. You look so straight and sober and weighted with cares. Remember the days when we had nothing more perilous to decide than whether to see the movie at the Bijou or the Strand? (Eventually we saw them both anyway.) Do you ever want to go back? Stupid! We can't.

I've been amusing myself by analyzing your February horoscope. You are—

1. An all-around person, specializing in nothing. (Hmmn—paints, plays the piano, takes photographs, writes well, good swimmer. Accurate?)
2. Fond of imparting knowledge to others. (You certainly like to convince me you're right.)
3. Excellent teacher, good surgeon, poor mathematician. (Aunt Marie always saw you as a university professor.)
4. Kind, generous, courageous. (Yes, to deaf mutes and candy counter girls.)

5. Common sense stupendous, too practical to be visionary. (Yes, but last summer I detected something visionary as well.)
6. Never makes quick or drastic decisions, restrained and discreet. (True, too true.)
7. Good public citizen. (Ho, ho, ho.)

My weak hand faltereth. Give my love to your dear mother and father. I hope they both are well.

Love, Jennie

*   *   *

Wednesday, January 16, 1952

Jennie!

Pardon me whilst I mop a sweating brow. What a letter, your last! I had barely recovered from the news of your pneumonia when I came upon the list of marriage proposals up for your consideration. My god, girl, don't get married! What a horrible thing even to think of. If there is anything I abominate it is early marriages. All these bobby—socksers toddling off to their little split-level boxes which they immediately fill to bursting with drooling babies. Dorothy Jenkins next door got married to some ex-football hero with a crew-cut last Saturday and it was all I could do to summon up courtesy enough to kiss the bride. Don't sacrifice a glamorous career for the drudgery of the washtub and the basinette!!! Besides, your husband undoubtedly would not appreciate your tripping off every summer for your yearly tryst with me. Most of all, you don't belong to engineers and corporation lawyers, you belong—well, thank god, you said no.

Sorry those shots of me in uniform made you sad. Frankly, they don't lift my spirits either. I need not point out again that I have no fondness for ROTC or the Air Force. We now have the pleasure of choosing our "career fields." Flight Operations sounds impressive but one has to be able to see to apply, so it looks like Administration or Logistics for me. Far from the battlefield anyway. (My horoscope said courageous?)

Have I ever told you about my rich, Jewish friend Frank? He's odd—man-out here in goyland, naturally that makes me like him. I also like, frankly, driving around town with him in his yellow Cadillac convertible. His family runs some mysterious business out of their home. The other night he dragged me to his mansion to see a new teletype just installed in their living room. His large, dark, fiery mother was furiously sending and receiving messages, barking orders to Philadelphia, Omaha, St. Louis, and Denver when suddenly her voice grew shrill and she beckoned to Frank. He rushed to her side, she handed him a stack of money, he grabbed a little yellow book and me, and before I knew it we were roaring crosstown in the Caddy. We stopped in front of a run-down hovel with drawn shades. Frank instructed me to knock at the door, get the signature of the woman who answered, and hand her the money. Since beggars can't be chosers, I went. A tired looking woman of about thirty with her hair in pin—curls answered my knock, clutching a faded kimona together with both hands. She looked at the wad of money in my fist. "So the bitch is afraid to come herself, eh?" she sneered. I got her signature and beat a hasty retreat to the Cadillac, convinced I was involved in a nation-wide vice syndicate. Frank offered no explanation.

Dreadful guests came to call this evening. A Mr. Bradley ("Just call me Wally, son") and his wife. I could hardly bear the hours I was forced to listen to the exploits of his son at Yale, but when he accused me of being a no-good loafter because I take nothing but art courses—and my dad agreed—I could hardly restrain myself from throttling him on the spot. What a wind bag. My poor mother didn't even get a chance to talk about her operation. She was very pleased, not incidentally, with the elegant rose-scented soap you sent and is writing to say so.

And now I shall roll over, snap off the light and dream. Perhaps of you. I am so lonesome and you are so far away and summer seems so remote.

So please write soon—

Much love, Rob

*   *   *

Sunday, January 27, 1952

Dear Rob,

I just got a letter from Donald so juvenile that it brought to mind the days we would sneak down Delavan alleys only to be confronted at their end by "Saaay, Robbie "in that deadly nasal drawl. Quote from letter: "My dear, have I informed you that I am now an uncle? She is really a beautiful little tyke and I must admit I'm very fond of the mischievous little rouge." Don't you suppose he means rogue? Looks like his sister Bitsy is married (at least we hope so). Wonder if she got her millionaire. Mr. Lindsay will disown her if she didn't.

Contrary to your assumption, I would not be tied down to bassinets and washtubs even if I did get married. I would talk the lawyer into taking me on as his partner and the chemical engineer into hiring me as an assistant. Or I would stay home and write thrilling novels. No, that's not the hitch of marriage. What bothers me (this is in the form of a confession, Rob) is maybe having to satisfy the desires of someone I didn't love. I don't think I could bear it. Far too much Grandmother and too little Freud. Anyway, our yearly visits simply must continue—even over my husband's dead body. But there!—I don't have a husband.

HAPPY, HAPPY BIRTHDAY!

Darling, remember the day I proposed to you? Wasn't that a lovely day?

Comparing it with these days, spent in a reeking lab sketching pickled frogs, hydra, ocotpi, and some unidentified fresh young thing. Our lab instructor bears a startling resemblance to the fifth bottle, fourth row in the cabinet of horrors, labeled ELASMOBRANCHII VULGARIS. It is. He is. Oh god, what's the use of this!

I laughed out loud over your letter. Someday we must write our memoirs. I bid for the Sunday three people went tearing around Milwaukee in a car none of them knew how to drive, scattering pedestrians in all directions when you leaned out the window and shouted "Look out! I can't find the brakes!" But you had better write them, you are the wit. Perhaps I could type—ah, but then you do that better too.

Did I tell you I am learning to fly in eight easy lessons? Just think—with your logistics and my pilot's license we can take off into the blue . . . away . . . no highway in the sky.

Much love, Jennie

*　　*　　*

Sunday, February 10, 1952

Dear Jennie,

Thanks for the birthday wishes. I am nineteen. Have pity, what an awful age! Soon I'll have to start lying about it.

I think it's exciting you're taking flying lessons. How thrilling it will be for me, a private first class in the U.S. Air Force Reserve Officers Training Corps, to know a genuine aviatrix. Let's fly to some little spot in South America this summer. Or maybe Cuba. We could explore the old caves of the Incas—maybe I could pick up some souvenirs for art history. Think I'm kidding? I'm not. Let's do it whether you're at the controls or not.

Between semesters, Drake University has deteriorated drastically. Deadly dull. I have been saddled with some of the most unfortunate human beings for teachers. Take Art History. The teacher has travelled far and wide, has friends in high places, is young of age and fair of face. Yet the art of teaching completely eludes her. We sit in a cold, damp classroom from eight to nine three mornings a week and listen to her drone. The correct answer to everything is "Increased interest in anatomy, aerial and linear perspective, application of color, and effect of light and shade." Teacher goes into little fits of ecstasy every time one of her students says this, for it shows we are learning to "think for ourselves." I just bundle into my coat, drowse off, mumble the formula when called on, and drift back to sleep while she chalks up an A.

English is worse because it occurs later in the day and by that time I am fully awake. Somewhere along the line we have slipped back into fifth grade. Currently we are wrestling with the simple sentence and the comma splice. Only four of us in class are literate; discontented with the simple prattle around us, we sit in the back and discuss Sex and Death while the professor drills the retarded in the use of the semi-colon.

So far the high point in psych class has been a thrilling movie on human reproduction. Father reading the newspaper, eight-year-old son playing on living room floor. Son crawls over, pokes father. Son: "Daddy, where do babies come from?" Daddy, vaguely worried, hoists son on knee. Daddy: "Well, I really don't know the answer to that, son." Narrator's voice over: "That's right, Dad, you don't know. But don't you think it's time you learned?" Everyone agreed it was high time.

I must retire now—if I can. The house is crowded with all my parents' most obnoxious friends. They always invite the obnoxious ones in a big bunch to get it over with. As you can see, my mother has quite fully recovered.

Much love, Rob

P.S. You don't mention Grandmother any more. Is she still kicking?

*   *   *

Wednesday, February 27, 1952

Dear Rob,

Life is beginning to look up again. Four new possibilities have appeared on the horizon. First: my uncle just asked me to fly to Washington to visit him this spring vacation. Will I. Second: Aunt Marie introduced me to a Milwaukee friend who happens to be the person who hires models at Gimbels. I think I have a job modeling if I want it! Gimbels model! Third: Uncle John asked us to choose between Mexico and Cuba as a little jaunt this summer. Will we. Fourth: Aunt Marie offered to finance six weeks of art lessons this summer at Milwaukee's Layton Art Institute. Yes. What will you be doing this summer, Rob? Perhaps we could stop for you on our way to Mexico? Elsie's dying to see you again, having barely been introduced last summer in Milwaukee. I say nothing of myself.

You asked about Grandmother. Since we're blocks out of reach I feel fairly free from her terrors. I'm afraid that Aunt Marie, who came home after our flight, had to take a great deal of abuse. And Grandmother is still highly capable of making trouble. Last Christmas Eve we were forced to assemble and open presents around the tree. Uncle John pulled out a toy train. Grandmother went off into obscene laughter. "Boys who never grow up get toys!" You can imagine with what enthusiasm the rest of us opened our gifts. Mother got a soap bubble pipe, my grandfather a donkey that kicked its hind legs when you pulled a string, and I a child's mirror, lipstick, brush and comb—"A vanity set," Grandmother informed me. Aunt Marie's was the worst: baby dolls in a cradle. Uncle John tried passing the whole thing off as a joke—"Isn't Mother witty!"

I know Grandmother is the reason Marie and John never married and that my mother is divorced. Her mission is to poison all wells.

Your stories of high school—college, pardon me—are all too familiar. How do these incompetents get hired? My French teacher is really a biologist, while my European history teacher specializes in American and thinks European utterly decadent. You can imagine with what enthusiasm he teaches the class.

Please do write soon. I did. (This little phrase used to touch me deeply when you wrote it and usually inspired a prompt reply.)

Love, Jennie

*   *   *

Sunday, March 9, 1952

Dear Jennie,

Just a short note. Although 'tis very late and I am half-dead with fatigue, your touching "write soon, I did" reached my heart.

I was in a horrible mood when your last letter came, but it was so chock full of jolly good tidings that I couldn't help brightening up. You are evidently going to have a busy and glorious summer. Made more glorious, may I add, by my presence with you in far-off Mexico. I have already packed my swimming trunks and camera (what more is needed?) and will be eagerly waiting for you to sweep by and pick me up this summer.

Of course, you MUST become a model at Gimbels. I shall come for lunch with one of my old Milwaukee flames, buy her a shrimp cocktail (no, on second thought she'll buy her own), and then we shall lean back and drink in the beauty of the models sauntering by. One glamorous creature will strike my fancy, I will stop her, ask her to turn around slowly. I will gaze at her with amorous eyes, my old flame will burn with jealousy. Yes, you must—you really must.

Sorry, darling, but I agree with Uncle John: "Mother is witty"!

School is just the same as when I last wrote. Instead of drawing biology lab skeletons in art class we are now sketching from a live model. Since he is a man of about 100, simply a bag of skin and bones, my new drawings look remarkably like the old. Art History has reached Michelangelo whose work is considerably more inspired than most we have studied, and hallelujah, I'm making A's in English in spite of rarely going to class.

Will use this space to humbly beg a speedy reply and send my love Rob

*   *   *

Sunday, March 23, 1952

Dear Rob,

Over my dead body will you take someone else to Gimbels for shrimp cocktails. Shrimp cocktails at Gimbels belong to us, as does Marietta House, a particular stretch of Milwaukee beach, an antique shop in Des Moines, and a lake path in Delavan. Should you dare take anyone else to these hovels of memory I shall be horribly violated. I do hope Mexico or Cuba will become another hovel of memory, and I'm so glad you're ready.

I hope we can get together with Donald again this summer. I do wish we'd been nicer to him all these years. Of course, this is easy to say with miles between us and hard to do when face to face. I remember when I used to consider you a creature of mystery and awe. I looked at you as I would an exhibit or a very amusing comedy act—someone to be entertained by, but not someone I could ever know or understand. You were so utterly out of reach. I don't mean to be at all insulting. You are still interesting—toujours, but a little more human now.

A sublime mix-up came my way yesterday. I wrote a letter to Sandy at Downer just mentioning Richard Behrens from Stanley (I think I've told you about him. He got drafted into the Army last December and plies me with letters). Sandy wrote her ancient grandmother in Stevens Point that I am going with Richard Behrens. Ancient grandmother remembers "going with" means "engaged," totters to phone and calls Richard's mother to congratulate her on his engagement. Richard's mother promptly calls me long distance wondering why her boy hasn't told her the happy news. Wants me to have her diamond as an engagement ring. Had the most agonizing time trying to explain, hung up in a cold sweat. I still have the ghastly feeling that somewhere, somehow, I may be engaged.

Comes spring and the usual yearning to be up and off to new lands. You know me—always searching, never finding. Someday I'm going to find it—or else! Or else? I'm beginning to entertain visions of a peaceful spinsterhood with many cats. There are worse things, I suppose.

Margot Peters

I'm off to Washington in two weeks. In preparation I've read Truman's book. Poor man, my heart bleeds for him. Really, being president must be such a trial. Speaking of politics, Taft is due here tonight, Stassen tomorrow, and Warren Saturday. Can't stand any of them but will go hear them for history credit.

Do you love "Blue Tango"? I'm mad, MAD over it.

Love, Jennie

*　　*　　*

126

Saturday, April 5, 1952

Dear Jennie,

Three things are always white: the wedding cake, the flag of truce, and the lining of a coffin.
M. Polychoff

Marriage: when two people under the influence of the most violent, most insane, most delusive and most transient of passions are required to swear that they will remain in that excited, abnormal and exhausting condition until death them do part.
—George Bernard Shaw (who else!)

I do not feel obliged to explain why I am passing on to you the above words of wisdom.

Was it a big let-down when you found out I was human after all? Really, I'm rather sorry you no longer consider me mysterious. What can I do to restore the illusion? Next time I see you shall I wrap myself in flowing black robes and whisper incantations in a foreign tongue, or shall I take a vow of silence and only gaze at you mutely with liquid dark brown eyes, or shall I perhaps dye my hair blue and start painting with my feet? Or shall I simply come with Muriel in tow—Muriel who reports that she has lost ten more pounds for love of me and is flunking all her classes in the exclusive girls college to which she has been confined by her furious parents who cannot bear to think of their precious, wealthy Jewish daughter in love with a German boy named Falkner from Des Moines.

This weekend Des Moines got a touch of spring. All the neighbors came streaming out of their houses bearing rakes, ladders, paint brushes, grass seed, clippers, etc. Fires were the order of the day and soon a pall of smoke hung over the neighborhood, obliterating the spring air. We all spent the weekend worrying lest my father collapse. He planted grass seed, raked the lawn, shoveled dirt, painted the back hall and the basement, and sawed dead limbs. In the middle of our lawn stands a Chinese elm. At its top hangs a broken branch, threat to all who pass underneath. My father spoke: "Down it must come."

Since the branch was too high to reach with poles and too dangerous to climb after, my father devised a weighted clothesline. This in theory he would cast over the branch and tug until the thing came tumbling down. He cast, he pulled. The tree groaned and began to lean westward, but the branch did not budge. Instead the rope broke, leaving the weights and most of the clothesline in the tree. Soon the elm looked like a Christmas tree decorated with dozens of rope ends and weights. Crowds of neighbors gathered to watch the titanic struggle. By suppertime the victory still lay with the branch. I expect the battle will be resumed tomorrow.

My exertions won me the twenty-five dollar popular art award. Of course I shall wonder the rest of my days whether I would have won if I hadn't hustled friends, neighbors, and strangers down to the Center to vote. This week our exhibit has been replaced by an exhibition of paintings done by patients in mental institutions. I'm afraid the general public won't see any difference between this week and last.

I'm enclosing a clipping about the show. That's me with the winning painting. Actually, my life drawing class professor tells me I'm very good, even very very good. He keeps urging me to flee Drake U. for the Chicago Art Institute, where all serious budding artists go. Shall I? I would be nearer by 100 miles, my goddess, to thee.

Have a wonderful time in Washington. Don't forget to drop me a post card. The Eiffel Tower, Grant's Tomb, apple blossoms along the Nile—who's particular.

Much love, Rob

* * *

Wednesday, April 9, 1952

Dear Rob,

I am sitting under a white dogwood tree at the Shoreham Hotel. An occasional breeze blows through the fountain and shakes a shower of blossoms at my feet. Another beautiful morning.

When I arrived last Friday at midnight, Uncle John picked me up at the airport and we went straight to the Shorewood Hotel's Palladium Room and listened to a marimba band until 2:30. What a different world, what a different uncle! He's the Shoreham's public relations director and seems to exist in a social whirl, and now I too am part of it!

Next day we went to a hunt meet in Virginia. Riders' pinks and glossy horses foreground, white fences blue mountains back. Afterwards a cocktail buffet at an old Virginia estate—Negro servants, an assemblage of admirals, Southern colonels, and horsemen, and the current Washington beauty with a figure like a packed hourglass, surrounded all evening by a stable of men. And me. I was petrified into silence at first, but was temporarily rescued by somebody also named McAllister, who probed my family tree (shades of Donald's father). Of course I had nothing to say about my family tree. Finally I was befriended by an aging opera singer with a black monocle, who invited me to tea at her Georgetown home.

Monday evening we dined with the editor of The Diplomat, a Washington society magazine. This man, Monty Radlovik, is about 39, has a fascinating accent, and is handsome in a kind of smoldering eastern European way. By the end of the evening, he declared he had fallen in love with me, asked me to become co-editor of the "Ambassador" and proposed marriage—the works.

Naturally it was hard to take him seriously. He is a bosom buddy of my uncle's. I don't think he knows how old I am. He is rather charming—the hand-kissing type, gallant. My uncle conveniently disappeared after dinner and Monty drove me around Washington for hours. Last evening he took me to Michele's, a gloomy cellar with gypsy music, good wine, and ATMOSPHERE. Tonight we are going to hear the Philadelphia Symphony at Constitution Hall.

Of all coincidences. I was sitting in the Shoreham lobby yesterday when who should come waltzing in but Sarah Conner! She is staying at the Shoreham too. I had no inkling of this, but her father used to be a Senator, and she has relatives in Virginia and family friends in Washington. (Amazing, truly, the things I don't know.)We immediately headed for cocktails in the Blue Room, and chewed over the good old times.

Got to meet Uncle John and Monty now. Will write more when I return to Wausau. Here comes Connor—she bids you a passionate hello.

Much, much love, Jennie

Later: Have met Senator McCarthy, Omar Bradley, Mr. and Mrs. Wiley, Gwen Caffritz (the hostess), the editor of the Times Herald, Mr. and Mrs. James Justice Burton, the French Ambassador, Paul Hume, etc. etc.

*   *   *

Friday April 11, 1952

Once again it is Friday evening in Des Moines and NBC presents LETTER FROM JENNIE. And now the radio program that asks the question: "Can a young girl from a small skiing settlement in northern Wisconsin find happiness at the center of Washington's mad social whirl?"

As you remember, Jennifer, her hair dyed midnight blue to impress the ardent Count Osculant, has just arrived in our nation's capital. Will her wild scheme to attract Osculant succeed? And what about Morty Lickovac, handsome editor of the "Ambassablast," who has been pursuing her passionately in Yugoslavian? Does he suspect the fact that our girl does not understand a syllable of the language? Who is the mysterious opera singer who is too obviously trying to lure our heroine to her mansion, and what dark purpose lies behind her sudden friendship? Can we trust General McAllister's claim to be our Jennifer's long-lost seventeenth cousin, or does he secretly want to show our heroine the family jewels. Can it be coincidence that the notorious Sarah Connor is found at Jennifer's hotel, or will this appearance of a leaf from her past prove a harbinger of doom? Will Michele's cellar finally prove her undoing? And WHAT UNFORSEEN IMPACT will these intrigues have upon Bor Renklaf, languishing forsaken in an Iowa cornfield? Don't miss a single second of the exciting drama, LETTER FROM JENNIE.

Sweetheart, it's getting good. Hurry and send me the next chapter.

While you are being toasted in the nation's capital, I too have been leading a glamorous existence. I marched in the Drake Relays Parade yesterday, one of 600 ROTC men to parade three miles down the avenue in winter wool uniforms during an 80 degree heat wave. (Yet there is something about 600 blue uniforms marching along to the strains of "Wild Blue Yonder" that is rather impressive, even if one is out of step.) I also went to a movie. Dear, if you have never been to a movie you must try it sometime. You enter this enormous cavern. It's black as pitch and there are other people there too. In front of you is a huge rectangle with people MOVING and TALKING on it. You stare at this rectangle and eat popcorn and watch people shoot each other and kiss. See, I've been having a whirl too.

Honestly, though, Washington sounds like fun, and I am losing sleep worrying about you and Morty.

Much love, Bor

*   *   *

Monday, April 14, 1952

Another LETTER FROM JENNIE:

We find our heroine at a race track in Maryland, Madlavic at her side. They are toasting each other in mint juleps—ah, she has just won $20 on number 7. Our heroine is in raptures—now she can buy the wretch in the cornfields a Washington souvenir. Fortunately, Madlavic has not guessed the reason for her joy or things would not be well for Jennie.

A reception for the Cuban ambassador. His Excellency has presented our Jennie with a copy of his new book and invited her to Cuba for the winter—in Spanish, of course. Ah, a menacing shadow looms on the scene—it is Manto Lackoluc, green with envy. He strolls past, frowning darkly at His Excellency's shoulder. At first opportunity, he seizes our heroine's arm and hisses, "REMEMBER, YOU ARE MINE!" Jennie seems to be having a hard time remembering.

Monto and Jennie are clasping hands over a table in Old New Orleans, a romantic little nightclub charging a romantic $15 for a glass of champagne. Our heroine seems ill at ease. She tries desperately to free her hand, but Monto will not be dissuaded. They dance. He blows hot air into her ear. He orders more champagne. He proposes bed. She refuses. He proposes a penthouse overlooking Rock Creek Park. She declines a taste for heights. He proposes marriage. Before our poor heroine knows quite what she has done, she seems to have promised to be Ridlovak's wife! She thinks sadly of the poor wretch languishing in the cornfields. She wishes to heaven she were languishing there too. Life has become DAMNED complicated.

Well, darling, there's the second installment. All resemblances to actual names, places, and events is rather accurate. What am I doing?

Aunt Marie has suggested I go to summer school in Milwaukee and I agree. I'll be staying at our Marietta House, home of the laughing furnace, the twin grand pianos, and the spiral staircase. Now you WILL come to Milwaukee, won't you? Elsie once accused me of being too forward with you, but can it be wrong to say right out that I want to see you again? A small chance that I may have Uncle's robin's egg blue Packard convertible to use while there. Summer school starts June 22, ends August 1. Well, it's up to you. All I can do is pray you'll come. So much to talk to you about. So want to be with you again.

Much, much love,
Jennie

* * *

Wednesday, April 16, 1952

And now, listeners, it's time for another spine-tingling chapter of LETTER FROM JENNIE. As you recall, our girl had wildly accepted a proposal of marriage from the sinister Menty Lackovic though torn by remorse for the innocent in the cornfields. Her life had become terribly entangled and the way seemed dark indeed. Sensing danger, however, and viewing aghast Jennie's wild spree, her maiden aunt has descended in a cloud of wrath and bore Jennie off to seclusion in the cloistered halls of a scholarly academy. Little does Auntie suspect, however, that the desperate girl has already dispatched a message to the wretch in the cornfields entreating him to join her in those same sanctified halls. Is our heroine aware that he plans to accept her invitation? What dastardly deed may Munty commit if he discovers Jennie's perfidy? Will implacable forces prevent our hero from trysting with our heroine, or will he be carried safely to his love . . . ?

At least he will be carried safely as far as Delavan—just heard today that we'll be there the whole month of June. Somehow the place has lost most of its charm for me, pin-up Muriel and all. At least I'll be close to Milwaukee. Naturally I'm wild to visit you—who wouldn't be: fascinating woman, fascinating Marietta House, fascinating blue Packard—perhaps.

God only knows what I'll actually end up doing this summer. I'm painting like mad and have signed up for classes at the Art Center in July. At the same time the Paramount people are pleading with me to take on a forty-hour week and more responsibility. I myself would like either to work on a road gang (I have a sudden passion for digging ditches—maybe it's the dollar an hour and the sunshine) or else happily fritter my time away in Milwaukee. Why don't you find me a job in Milwaukee so I can fritter to some purpose? Anyway, thanks for the invitation. Be assured I'll try to take you up on it—if you are not already married to Monty.

What would you like for your birthday next month? Shall I send you a self-portrait? Of course it hasn't been painted yet—patience, dear, the argylls, remember? Maybe I'll do one of you this summer at the wheel of the blue Packard convertible running down the common people, or sitting on a rock dangling your lovely feet in Lake Michigan. You name it.

Much love, Rob

* * *

May 11, 1952

'Tis Sunday evening, and NBC brings you the absolutely LAST LETTER FROM JENNIE. Yes, listeners, we have been banned in Boston, and not all your loyal enthusiasm can save our beloved heroine.

The scene is little Jennie's living room. She has just found four letters in the mailbox. Eagerly she rips open the first. It is from the wretch in the cornfields—ah, their Milwaukee rendezvous is set! Our Jennie bursts into tears of joy. She tears open a second letter from the Fort Delta infirmary. Poor Richard, whose mother still believes he and Jennie are engaged, has mumps and is wasting away. Jennie does not burst into tears of dismay. She rends the third. Monty Lackowit commands her to return to Washington immediately and marry him! Our heroine shudders. Warily she opens the fourth. Donald has not given up their love for lost and wants to try again this summer. Our Jennie shivers with horror.

Will Jennie find the cornfield wretch—despite his pretty words—still wretchedly cold when they meet? Will she fly to Richard's bedside to comfort him? Will she cast everything to the winds and become Radlovik's partner on The Amblassador and elsewhere? Will Donald win her at last, or will he die trying—murdered by our desperate girl?

I don't know, Rob, I simply don't know.

I've just had a superlative idea. Instead of taking art courses in Des Moines, come and take them with me in Milwaukee. The Layton School of Art is excellent, I hear. You could stay at Marietta House and you and Donald could get part-time jobs on a road gang. Now wouldn't that be fun?

Oh, yes—my birthday. What trifle would please me? Well . . . 1) to see you this summer, 2) to keep on receiving this flood of mail—don't know what has inspired it, but it's wonderful, 3) to have you paint me, 4) to let me paint you—temperamental egotist, dreamer with brown eyes, sunlight on a deep pool.

Better go feed the cat.

Much, much love, Jennie

*   *   *

Wednesday, May 14, 1952

Dear Jennie,

I don't know why, but I've suddenly developed a mania for the dance, so raided the library and carried off every book I could find on the subject. I'm now deep into Isadora Duncan's autobiography. She was either very great or horribly shallow. One can seldom tell. Anyway, so much she says could have been said by me—for example:

> From my earliest childhood I have always felt a great anti-pathy for anything connected with churches or church dogma.

> I am against the modern code of marriage, and I think the modern idea of a funeral ghastly and ugly to the degree of barbarism.

> It has been said that the first essential in writing about anything is that the writer should have no experience in the matter. Memories are less tangible than dreams.

> How can we write the truth about ourselves? Do we even know it? There is the vision our friends have of us; the vision we have of ourselves; and the vision our lover has of us. Also the vision our enemies have of us—and all these visions are different.

> I have sometimes been asked whether I consider love higher than art, and I have replied, I cannot separate them, for the artist is the only lover. He alone has the pure vision of beauty, and love is the vision of the soul when it is permitted to gaze upon immortal beauty.

Well, this could go on forever. My mother says she was a superb dancer, but insane.

A letter from Donald arrived today hand in hand with yours. He seems to be quite distraught about school, but I was encouraged that now at least he can spell it. Every other word was "taboo," as

Professor Munn of the Drake English Department blushingly puts it. I immediately hid the epistle lest it fall into the hands of my sister or mother. The two of us, he says, are going to "RAISE HELL!" this summer. Could be

I have suddenly—shades of Rembrandt and Van Gogh—become a painter of self portraits. Just finished a life-sized job. Took it to school. My classmates surround me in raptures. One goes so far as to take it off to a corner to contemplate for a full fifteen minutes. My professor is vastly impressed, but says I'm handsomer. I melt with delight. My dear friend Larry (you would love Larry: imagination, personality, one of the few people who finds humor in the same things I do—not safe to have us both in the same room at the same time), usually bitingly critical of my work, brings droves of people to view the masterpiece. Our model, whom I have loved from afar for many weeks, looks on in astonishment. I am perplexed by all the fuss, but run home and start a second. I have always considered the art of self—portrait a sign of colossal ego-mania, but now I suspect I'd better retract that opinion.

Can't wait till this summer. Stock sentence every spring. Hope to have more than a few fleeting hours with you. Want to just sit and draw, picnic in the country, swim on empty beaches, and walk and walk and walk. No movies, please! And minimal Donald.

My father tries to sleep, the typewriter disturbs him, mayhem is threatened if I go on.

WRITE.

Much love, Rob

*   *   *

Sunday, May 25, 1952

Dear Rob,

Isadora was a great dancer, a pathetic philosopher. I don't believe that the artist is the only lover. I don't believe that a pure vision of immortal beauty is the ultimate experience of love. What about kindness, loyalty, honesty, deep feeling—shouldn't they inspire love as much as "pure visions of immortal beauty"? She says you cannot write about that which you have experienced. I believe realism in writing comes from writing with passion of things felt, experienced or carefully observed. I distrust Isadora on literary matters—seems all her works were haunted by a ghost, so who is she to say? On the other hand, I absolutely agree with her about marriage and funerals.

Oh, summer sounds wonderful! How will we get out into the country, though? Blue Packard is fading fast. We'll have to take Donald and his car. I can draw you, you can draw Donald, and Donald can draw me. Since he tells me he is "blinded by my beauty" he will probably do the best job. I'm so glad you don't like crowded beaches any more. I used to complain about all the bodies on Bradford Beach and you always said that acres of half-naked humanity was fascinating. I also remember that at Delavan I was constantly trying to abduct you away to solitude, but that you always wanted Muriel, Roger, Carson, Pixie, Judy, Gingy, Barbara and the rest of the gang along too. So you like empty beaches. Well, well.

Whether or not you see me for more than a few fleeting hours is up to you. I'm getting a ride down with all my summer baggage June 12th, in time for Downer's graduation on the 13th—I must go. School doesn't start until the 23rd. You will be at Delavan all of June, so we have days and days to be with each other—if you choose. You know I do. Aunt Marie is "dorm sitting" Marietta House again, so the place is at your disposal—you may stay as many days as you like.

Congratulations on the success of the self-portrait. Do I get the second one? You promised

My aunt has found me a slight job reading to a blinded war veteran a few hours a week this summer, just like you did. Heaven knows, I can use the money, and may even learn something in the process.

Oh, all I can think of is this summer, and I'm not going to dwell on it.

Must take Grandfather to the baseball game now. It's the only thing he still likes to do.

Love, Jennie

*   *   *

Monday, July 7, 1952

Dear Rob,

I am sorry about last night. I did wait about 15 minutes, but then left. The reason I didn't wait longer? Seriously, I didn't think you would come. I didn't think you sounded enthusiastic over the phone about seeing me again so soon. Perhaps I should have more confidence, but it's hard. You always seem so casual about our meetings and promoting them that I hardly thought the long trip from Delavan was worth it to you for just one evening. That is what this summer did to me—I have become a creature of little faith.

I have been seeing a lot of Donald and his friends Pat Williams and Don Darnell. The latter seems intelligent though prone to bouts of hysterical laughter. The four of us went to the Catholic church last Sunday. Donald was always one step behind in genuflecting and crossing himself. We had to leave rather abruptly by a side door because Darnell went into fits of mirth at Donald's attempt at a Hail Mary.

That same day we lunched at the Lindsay mansion. I took my room mate along for Pat Williams, but neither spoke to each other all afternoon. Unfortunately, Donald took the occasion to show off his prowess at drinking. But I fixed him, maybe. He said, "Let's have a drink!" I said, "Fine. Make mine a double bourbon on the rocks." He looked appalled, but bravely poured himself a triple and downed it with a flourish. When his face had regained its normal hue, he offered me another, confident I would refuse. "Fine," says I. Another double and triple shot respectively. I finished mine, in pain. "One more, Donald—a toast!" cries I. Donald is fading fast away. "I don't think my old man would like it," he mumbles. "Give me hell when he gets home." I manage to look crestfallen. "Chicken," says Pat. "Here, bet you can't drink this beer." "You bastard," says Donald and chugs a Blatz. We left him in a stupor on the couch and went merrily on our way. It took me hours to recover, but was almost worth it.

I wish I could have said a proper "Auf Wiederzehn," but I'm sending you the record instead. "The time has come to part"—yes, again and again. If you can find it in your heart ever to write again after driving seventy miles in vain I shall be here until August 5.

Usually after we see each other we write furiously for a few months. This time you didn't so I can only conclude that you don't love me at all anymore. You don't, do you? I know it. And it could have been a GREAT THING.

Love and tears, Jennie

*   *   *

Tuesday, July 27, 1952

Dear Jennie,

My mother died five days ago. She seemed perfectly well at the lake, but when we got home, another tumor was discovered and she went downhill rapidly after that and was mercifully unconscious toward the end. My father is devastated. He always thought that because of his high blood pressure he would go first. He spends his days bewailing the fact that he never took her abroad, as she always begged him to, that he never learned to play bridge to please her, etc. etc. It is painful to hear.

The funeral was yesterday. I never knew we had so many relatives. There were at least 200 present from both sides of the family. Afterwards they all congregated inside the house and on the lawn to gorge themselves on a catered spread. Gingy, Cindy and I retreated to the basement and I was playing Shubert on the piano when my father stormed down and informed me I was being sacrilegious. Life with father may not be possible.

I'm just beginning to realize that my mother was probably my best friend. She always stood up for me and believed in me—with damned little encouragement.

Wanted you to know. She was very fond of you.

Love, Rob

*   *   *

Wednesday, July 28, 1952

Dearest Rob,

I tried three times to call you today, but no answer. I am so sorry about your mother that I can hardly write. Elsie is my best friend really, too. I think I'd die if I lost her. Oh, I'm so sad for you, and for Gingy and your father. It's the last thing I expected. You told me so positively that she was all better, and when I talked with her on the phone she sounded absolutely the same.

I'm in Milwaukee for another week. I know my aunt would lend me the money to fly to Des Moines. If you want me, I'll come. I know it's a terrible time for visitors, but I'd like to be with you—if you'd like me to be.

Please call me at Marietta House if I should come.

Much, much love, Jennie

*   *   *

Monday, December 1, 1952

MY LAST WILL AND TESTAMENT

In two weeks I shall be married. To Monty. If you dare reproach me I will remind you of the years I spent trying to talk you into a garret, a jug of wine and me. I failed miserably. But that's Jennie—always trying to infuse romance into a friendship that is inexorably a friendship, always pursuing what she can't have and throwing away what she can. Someday, when I'm famous, you will be able to say, "Ha, I scorned her love!" But then, you'll be the famous one.

Are you still a friend? Then you may be interested in the plans. Small wedding with only the magazine publisher and his wife in attendance. Two weeks honeymoon in New York. Live in Monty's apartment until spring when we will embark for for Europe. Buy a house in Chevy Chase when we return. Live.

I don't know what else to say. I'm not supposed to have any doubts, I realize, but of course I do. He loves me—or seems to—and will forgive. I hope.

I am not in any mood to write. If you would answer and tell me something then I would in turn know what to say. Say what you wish, but do say something. You haven't for a long, long time.

Love, Jennie

* * *

Wednesday, December 3, 1952

Well now, let's not get all excited about this. I'm not going to call you names, jump into the Des Moines river, or buy a gun and shoot Monty. Your letter somehow came as no surprise at all. I had been anticipating such tidings ever since you called last September and said you were returning to Washington.

The tone of your letter disturbs me no end. You sound more like the helpless heroine of one of those "marry me or I'll foreclose" melodramas than a happy bride. If you are doing this to ease the blow to me, stop, for god's sake, for the blow will be lighter if I think you are happy in your choice. If you really feel the way you seem to—well, if I were you, I wouldn't go through with the marriage for all the diplomats or trips to Europe or houses in Chevy Chase for the world.

Another thing that disturbs me in this business about my "scorning your love." That's laying it on a bit thick, don't you think? For one thing, I never knew it was mine to scorn . . . . your letters on the subject were seldom any more committal than mine. If I felt, however, that I had your love, I didn't encourage it, nor attempt to bind you in any way. Since we are necessarily separated most of the time, it would hardly be fair to either of us. You know how I feel about marrying young. I'm not ready to marry anyone yet. I'm not going to marry for at least five years. If it's any great joy to you to know this, I can say that you are the only girl I've ever considered as a wife, but I was not going to force the issue on the basis of five days together out of the 365. Nor did I want either of us to feel guilty if, as is quite conceivable, we should meet somebody else. You may feel differently, but I don't think a romance can be conducted by mail. It's been six months since we've seen each other. It has been I don't know how long since we've really been together any length of time—Delavan in 1950? Perhaps if we'd had more time together last summer things would have been different. I've meant to talk this out with you for some while; I guess I just didn't have the nerve. I didn't want to say wait for me—me, who regardless of what you say or think, you only know as someone who writes an amusing letter and sends you a picture once and a while. Nor did I dare say wait, hoping all along that perhaps you would.

Still, I'd be much happier if you had written, "Guess what? I'm going to be married! I'm thrilled to death about it. He's tall, dark, handsome and just my age. We won't be rich, but I love him!" I'd much prefer that to "I'm not supposed to have any doubts," "you scorned my love," "maybe he'll forgive." For god's sake, darling, if that's the way you feel don't go through with it! Do you want me to put on my maiden-rescuing outfit, and carry you off to our garret on your wedding night? I'd be more than happy to. Do you want me, when they say "Who has reasons to prevent this marriage?" to leap up and say "I do!" I will. Believe me, all the trips to Europe and New York, all the penthouses, all the mansions, won't be enough if you are really so unsure of your feelings.

How does your family feel about the situation? I dare say they are rather pleased.

Hope you will feel like writing. Hope Monty will not look askance at our correspondence. Hope you won't burn my letters. Think I will send you the big self-portrait as a wedding gift. You can hang it on the wall at the foot of your bed where I will smile down enigmatically upon your wedded bliss.

Wish you weren't getting married. Wish you weren't marrying MONTY.

Rob

* * *

New Year's Day, 1953

Dearest,

Can you forgive me for not letting you know what has happened?

I escaped once to Wausau, but seven phone calls from Monty convinced me that my decision had been too hasty, so I returned to Washington once more to reconsider.

The first day was heaven, then all the old arguments flared again. Nothing had changed. The climax came when Monty threw a tantrum in the Senate Restaurant over the famous bean soup. I told him he was an egomaniac who always had to have his way.

"I will always have my own way!" he shouted "My way is the right way!"

This confirmed old suspicions. They began one night when the Turkish ambassador said, "I do not let my wife go out to these—what do you call them—supermarkets. She is mine and I do not wish the public to look at her." My mouth fell open but Monty said, "Quite right. A woman belongs to her husband. These American women are shameless. We must teach them."

A Montenegrian teach an American! I thought the whole thing a joke at the time, but I have found out since—slowly, painfully—that Monty is impossible to please. He also plays the most sinister psychological games. One time he drew his car up to the curb saying, "There's the latest edition of the Post. Get out and buy it—I know you can't wait to read your name." "My name?" I said. "Yes, the guest list from Gwen Caffritz's party last night. Go on, buy the paper. You have been thinking about nothing else." I hadn't thought about it at all—it's he who's crazy to see his name in the society columns. Honestly, I think he's mad.

I left Washington again, this time not running but very deliberately.

Within four days, Monty was in Wausau, looking very tropical among our fur-wrapped peasants. I told him I would not return; he replied that in that case he would stay in Wausau. He marched off to buy a stadium coat and a fur cap with earmuffs like all the businessmen in town wear. Elsie was charmed.

I told him his wonderful magazine needed him and that if he would leave, I would seriously think about following.

He thought that over for a day, returned the stadium coat and earmuffs, and flew away.

When he called from DC I told him I wasn't coming until I grew up enough to know myself. I said that if he really loved me he would wait. He said that if I really loved him I would come. We left it at that.

Now that I am no longer an object of curiosity I suppose I don't rate the portrait. I would, however, hang it in my room at the University of Wisconsin next semester.

Please let me differ. Read Bernard Shaw and Ellen Terry. I think a romance can be conducted by mail. I think that's the best kind. I love your dear wonderful words. They are you as much as you are—why don't you know that?

I am reading a Christmas present, Charlotte Brontë's Villette, and having a wonderful time. You would hate it, but it must be the greatest novel ever written. Many many apologies for not answering your wire. As you see, things have returned to normal. I would welcome your forgiveness and a letter.

With love, Jennie

*   *   *

Monday, January 5, 1953

Dear Jennie,

How wonderful that you are out of the clutches of that dreadful man. Or are you? Perhaps he is once again in Wausau, perhaps you are once again in Washington. At least you can't say it hasn't been exciting.

I suppose you know that I am livid with rage at you! I have never felt so neglected as I did the weeks following that hour and a half phone call. How dare you stir up such a storm and then withdraw completely. I realize those were turbulent times, but all the same, Jennie, one little message, even a postcard, would have helped. How could you abandon me like that? When I didn't hear from you after I sent the wire, I was certain you had taken the fatal step, and draping your photographs in black, I retired to the piano and long sessions of Chopin's Funeral March and "Mood Indigo." Then I had a happy thought. Sure that your marriage would be doomed to failure, I decided to wait until the divorce and then run off with you to our garret and exist on your alimony. Though this cheered me a great deal, your letter saying you hadn't married Monty cheered me more.

I am decidedly pleased to hear that you are going back to school and descending from the heights of social Washington to the level of humdrum college life. I hardly need tell you what I think of society in general, and Washington society is beneath my contempt. Every time I read the "Ambassador" you sent I became more convinced of the worthiness of my ambition to become a hermit in outer Patagonia.

I am being very restrained in this letter as I still am not sure just how things stand in Wausau and our nation's capital. Nevertheless, I can't think of anything better for you than the University of Wisconsin this semester. I also think we must plan on seeing each other this summer, if not before.

All my love, Rob

*　　*　　*

Thursday, January 22, 1953

Ditch the drapes, darling. I'm free. Oh mad mad intoxicating freedom. Oh hosannas. Oh joy, la la la.

Yesterday I traded in my gowns and heels for a ski sweater, knee socks, camel's hair coat, saddle shoes and a plaid scarf. Soon I'll be collecting Bucky Badger dolls and Wisconsin beer steins. To hell with long white gloves and ambassadors and envoys and nightclubbing and champagne. Bucky Badger dolls for me, la la la.

Just for memories I've subscribed to the Washington Post and am a nervous wreck over the Indo-China crisis, the Italian coup, the Yugoslavian upheavals, the impending disaster in Germany and the tangle of the Bricker amendment. I fret for hours over Russia, France and NATO and EDC. Haven't sleep for nights. Oh gloom, la la la.

Please do not be restrained. When I think of Monty I think almost tenderly of that "pathetic old man." Of course, he's a skitso if not downright mad—but still, from this distance, he is just a sad, aging tyrant I was lucky enough to escape. Let us not speak cruelly of the dead. The Arab's citadel is buried in the sand. The sands may shift, baring ruins, but they are ruins.

My new address is Ann Emery Hall, Madison, after the 29th. La, la, la. I'll write more soon. And please, please write to me.

All my love, Jennie

P.S. DON'T TELL ME DONALD IS GOING STEADY. That's the news that met my weary eye as I opened his last letter. He is still talking about reunion. I would love a reunion. Without Donald. Just you, me, and the garret.

*　　*　　*

Saturday, February 21, 1953

Dear Jennie,

These are hectic times—I have to get paintings ready for no less than three shows in the next two months. This means painting three or four canvasses, building frames, painting frames, building crates, and shipping them. And of course I have to shine in all my regular classes at the same time.

Perhaps I will have a painting for you by your birthday . . . . I will try. What do you want? Surely not a self-portrait. That was only to hang over the double bed if you married Monty. I really am not egotistical enough to send even special young ladies Me by Me. You probably would hate my style anyway. Though conservative by present day standards, it's rather wild from the layman's point of view, and I must warn you that very few people—in fact only my art prof and I—like my paintings. My father won't have them in sight.

This year I've made an incredibly fast start on summer. Have a job lined up already at—you can't guess—the state mental hospital doing art therapy with the more tractable (I trust) patients. Seems that messing with finger paints and clay hath charms to soothe the savage breast, so I'm going to help them mess. Full time and a decent salary. I hope I hear faint cheers.

Yes, it appears that Donald is going steady. To me he confided, however, that "he could never get over you and is only glad that he is not losing you to me." How does he know he is not? You obviously haven't kept him up to date on the Washington saga.

Pray, what are these Bucky Badger dolls that you plan to collect? Stuffed or human? and what classes are you taking? Tell all. Do you realize I'm a full year ahead of you in college now? It gives me a feeling of the most immense superiority. The most paternalistic concern for your welfare.

But not enough energy to go on with this letter. It is two a.m. and tomorrow I must rise full of inspiration to attack an empty canvas. Write soon.

Much, much love, Rob

*   *   *

Saturday, February 28, 1953

Dear Rob,

What I went through waiting one month for your dear but one and a half page letter is not to be described.

Bucky Badger dolls are stuffed animals with red shirts, symbolic of this great universitatis luminatis. Campus wheels are also called Bucky Badgers, but they are large and hollow.

Classes? Logic, philosophy, Shakespeare's tragedies, contemporary lit and art history.

The logic professor is recovering from shellshock. The literature professor's eye rolls wildly as his hair stands on end. The philosophy professor has a club foot and falls off the platform regularly because he walks backwards as he writes on the board. The art history prof is perfect: suave, tall, greying, grey flannels. Haven't missed art history yet.

To my great surprise I found myself sitting next to old Jim Brandt from Wausau in my philosophy class. You probably don't remember old Jim.

No sorority for me. Elsie can't afford it, I don't want it. That leaves me with the GDIs, I guess.

I'd heard that you can't get along at the U if you don't swill beer. I've always hated the stuff, so I grit my teeth and prepared to be unpopular. Seems, however, there's always someone with a hip flask who thinks you're too cute if you help him drain it, so I'm not as out of it as I thought. My social life right now is bewildering. I spend half my time talking LIFE with strange characters in the Rathskellar and the other half partying with fraternity lads who creep in white bucks. Jim wears white bucks. Wouldn't you know.

Please write soon and tell me more about your arty world and I'll tell you more about my childish one. Healthy, yes—but all I can think when I occasionally run into my little sorority-bound roommate is, "And you think you've lived!"

Wonderful about the summer job—"Save some for Virginia!" I do envy you, your painting, your certain career and all. What am I going to do with Shakespeare?

Much love, Jennie
The phone just rang. It was Sandy Erwin. She's engaged to Jack Rees. Good grief.

* * *

Sunday, March 15, 1953

Dear Rob,

I must write you a note although I haven't heard from you. The reason? A friend of mine who lives in Madison is leaving with her family for Florida over spring vacation, April 6 to 14. What has this to do with us? Our garret! She has offered me the apartment if I want it. I do want it—if you could possibly come. Can you? When is your spring vacation? You must come, I do want it so much. And with your job who knows whether we will ever be able to see each other this summer? Oh, it will be a purely platonic little garret, don't fear. No scandals—nevah! I'm in a rush for philosophy class, but had to tell you.
Do write.

Much love, Jennie

*   *   *

Thursday, October 7, 1954

Dear Rob,

I think this is the hardest letter I've ever had to write. I've postponed it for more than a year. You can probably guess what inspired me to communicate at last. My aunt ran into Donald who said he had heard from you asking about me. I tore up your last letter to me. I couldn't read it and I couldn't answer. But now I must.

Rumors are true. I am married, to Jim. For quite some time now, which is fortunate seeing that I have a small son. His name is Mark (after nobody) John (after my uncle). It is true too that I had to get married. Elsie never talked about realities. It's hard to tell you this, but I wasn't a virgin anyway. Monty took care of that. How you must deplore me.

Nothing's wrong with my marriage except I don't love my husband, and never really did, I believe now.

I know what you're thinking: "Why that crazy, fabulous, interesting creature has got herself plumb into the midst of another melerdrama." Please don't think that. I haven't.

There are a hundred things to tell you but I'll skip them. The fact is, I'm planning to move to Madison rather soon, find an apartment, get a job, and divorce my husband.

"Ah, a gay divorcée! How I love 'em."

Please don't.

I had planned on getting an apartment with Connor, who is sane, single, smart, and going to the U this fall. Unfortunately, her parents, who are strict Catholics, absolutely forbid it on the grounds that she would be party to the breaking up of a happy home.

She can't defy her parents because they're supporting her through school, so I'm on my own. I'm finding it rather hard to find a job "long distance" as it were, for Richland Center is sixty miles from Madison and I don't often have a car to use. And rents are so high in Madison that I wonder how I'll be able to manage.

Funny isn't it, how people can concentrate on such trivia. My whole life is a mess and I'm talking to you about high rents. Perhaps because simple economics has become my chief occupation of late.

Please, if you can find it in your heart, write me. Tell me all the interesting things you're doing. Are you graduating this semester? Are you in love? Married? Famous? Assure me there are Brighter Days Ahead. New horizons. A year and a half in this clutchy, cliquey town is enough to suffocate anyone. And to have to pretend and pretend and smile and smile is too hard to bear sometimes.

Consider a letter to me your Duty. Operation Lost Soul.

Jennie

*   *   *

Sunday, October 10, 1954

Dear Jennie,

I had heard about your marriage, but vaguely, as something guessed at rather than known. Jim. And Mark John. And Richland Center. You seem very far away.

I'm afraid I don't have Connor's parents' scruples about the breakup of homes. If you are unhappy, Jennie, then I suppose you must leave. Have you tried to stick it out and make the best of things? But I know nothing of the situation. Jim is just a shadow, your old knight in shining armor, now evidently rather tarnished.

(Please let's not discuss the hows and whens of your lost virginity. Frankly, my dear, I don't give a damn. Besides, now we're even.)

All will depend, as you know, on your finding a job. Does Jim know you want to leave? If he doesn't, if you have to steal away to Madison on the sly, then it will be difficult. I hate to mention this because we disagree, but what about Aunt Marie? She has helped you with school and finances in the past. She has your welfare at heart—almost more than your mother, I believe, though I know she has often antagonized you. Can't you appeal to her for help? What about Milwaukee instead of Madison? Why does it have to be Madison?

Could we possibly see each other again? I'm at the Chicago Art Institute now (I graduated a semester early and am here on a scholarship working on a master's). On October 29, Friday, I have no classes and am planning to stay with relatives in Milwaukee for the weekend. I could come to Madison Saturday and you could meet me there. But I only suggest this if the situation warrants it. Please use your best judgment.

Gingy is a college sophomore at Drake right now—rather hard to believe. Dad and I have had a rough time. He went into deep depression after Mother died; as matter of fact, I was not unshaken myself. We barely spoke to each other for almost a year. And then—as you know—he has never reconciled himself to an artist for a son. But one day last spring he left a folder on my desk which proved to contain a sheaf of poetry he had written. Actually I was amazed: the stuff was quite good. Glad I could tell him that. It was his way of trying to bridge the gap, and things have been less antagonistic since.

What to say about myself? The Institute is fairly challenging. There are a few inspiring teachers. I'm applying for a Fulbright to study abroad. I share a large ramshackle house on Armitage we call the Chateau Ninevah with six males. It is dominated by a large, fuzzy—haired man named Staube, who has indoctrinated me into the beauties of Wagner and Richard Strauss. Currently I am wild about "Salomé" and "Verklarte Nacht." Such a wholesome creature, Salomé.

You remember Muriel from the lake, don't you? The poor child who had a crush on me? She wasn't out last summer, so mainly to be polite, I asked about her. At first Mrs. Rosen would not speak to me; eventually she confided that Muriel is incarcerated in a private hospital outside Milwaukee. When I expressed concern, Mrs. Rosen said, "Then go visit her." Felt I had to go. The hospital let me stay half an hour. Muriel is a wizened gnome weighing about sixty-five pounds. She is dark brown, like a shriveled nut. She is in a wheelchair with tubes in her arms—the only way she takes nourishment. You would not recognize her. Can't remember how I got through the half-hour, just remember stumbling out into the sunshine again. But worse was to come. Mrs. Rosen called me over to their place to ask how the visit had gone. Before I could tell her, she said, "You know, of course, that she is starving herself to death for you."

The terrible thing is, I believe it may be true. She was always chasing me, in a good-girl sort of way, and I probably was just nice enough to encourage her without intending to encourage her at all. She may die.

Let me know about the 29th. Does Jim read your letters? Perhaps you'd better burn this one.

Love, Rob

*   *   *

Saturday, October 16, 1954

Dear Rob,

I am deeply touched by your willingness to help. That sounds so stiff and formal, but I remember that in the past it was always me who kept asking "When can we see each other again?" and now you seem to want to see me and it's such a lovely change. I have a sneaking suspicion it may just be morbid curiosity on your part, but I'm grateful. You won't be afraid of me, will you? I haven't changed much except I don't lie anymore. Those flying lessons, remember? Otherwise expect the same Jennie. I seem to go through fire and flood outwardly unscathed, though heaven knows what's happening inside.

October 29 is not far off. I must plan carefully. I can be in Madison certainly all day Saturday. I will pay Jim five dollars for the car (we have a company car and it costs four cents a mile), that way I won't feel the trip's on him. If I come only for Saturday there won't be complications—I will just tell Jim I'm going to look for a job. He knows about this—I've done it in the past. If I stay overnight I'll have to think up a good story. Of course that's my problem, so don't worry. What about meeting Saturday morning in Madison. I think I can stay over till Sunday. Can you? Let me know.

Graduate school, a Fulbright—how exciting. Have you decided to be an art scholar or an artist? Surely the latter. I still entertain the misguided notion that I can be a writer if I put my mind to it, and am currently sending stories to McCalls or the Ladies Home Journal. Such tripe they print, how I wish I could produce same. On the other hand if they'd accept a story I'd grovel. I have a small job now, two evenings a week—teaching guitar. Two of my pupils are better than I am.

Of course I remember Muriel. I used to think sometimes you loved her better than me. Perhaps you did, what? What a horrible thing, starving herself! But Rob, surely it wasn't just you. You told me that her parents wouldn't hear of her falling in love with someone non-Jewish. This could very well be Muriel's revenge against her parents, not you. Must talk about this when we meet.

Speaking of Salomé, there's another opera about the wholesome creature you might like to look up—"Herodias" by Massenet. The high spot is the aria "Il Est Doux, Il Est Bon," sung by Salomé of John the Baptist. When Grace Moore soars into "Propheté, bien-aimé, puis je vivre sans toi" I go into ecstasies. Of course, Grace isn't exactly first-class—a little breathy—but the aria is glorious. What a joy to talk about these things again. (Incidently, why do you—cool and composed—like wild composers like Rachmoninoff, Liszt, and Wagner, while I—a raving romantic—like cool composers like Bach, Haydn, and Mozart?)

Do answer soon and tell me when you'll come. I'm very excited about seeing you again, and very grateful for your kindness.

Jennie

*   *   *

Monday, October 18, 1954

Dear Jennie,

Glad you want to come. Personally, Friday and Saturday would be best for me. I should be back in Milwaukee for Sunday dinner and then there's the bus ride back to Chicago and school at eight the next day. Don't worry about finding a place to stay overnight. Perhaps we could drive back to Milwaukee and stay at my relatives' and haunt the old spots all days Saturday. If not, surely there are rooms in Madison. If we stay in Madison, I insist we spend the day hunting jobs for you.

Bring your bathing suit and camera—no, it's not summer any more, is it. But I expect you to find a piano and play "Il Est Doux" for me and I shall return the favor with a stormy rendition of Beethoven's "Appasionata."

A terrible thought just struck me. You are taking the company car. But can you drive? You'll forgive me if the memory of you abandoning the wheel in the midst of Milwaukee's busiest intersection still haunts me.

Till Friday then, I trust.

Much love, Rob

* * *

Friday, October 22, 1954

I haven't haunted the mailbox since the old days when I'd wait for the first letter after Delavan. Such romance, such intrigue. Such nervous prostration . . .

I think the Friday to Saturday plan is best too. The earliest I can possibly meet you would be about five Friday afternoon. Jim usually gets home about four and it takes an hour to get to Madison. So let's say I'll meet you between five and five-thirty in the lobby of the Loraine Hotel five days from today. You undoubtedly know where the Loraine is; if you don't it's right across the street from the bus station.

I must be back Saturday evening. I would love to stay longer, but I guess we have to snatch at straws. I'm just terribly happy that we can see each other at all.

I haven't decided yet whether I will just leave on Friday, pinning an explanatory note in some conspicuous place, or whether I should tell Jim beforehand that I'm going to Madison to see Connor and look for a job. I'd prefer the latter, but I'm afraid he might not let me have the car. If I insisted, he'd hide the car keys. Afraid I'll have to sneak. How to get out of the house leaving a child and a hungry husband will be a problem to occupy me for the coming days.

But I'll be there.

We can decide about Milwaukee later. I'd rather stay in Madison except there are a dozen people I know well who'll probably turn up there at the same time. The last time I shopped in Madison I ran into an old friend from Wausau, had coffee with him at the Hotel Loraine, and all Richland Center chose to be there and report back to Jim that day. Perhaps we can frequent out of the way spots. Or shall we be brave.

My driving has progressed somewhat since Milwaukee. They'd never have given me a license if it hadn't.

Till Friday then.

Jennie

*   *   *

Friday, November 5, 1954

Dear Rob,

It's now almost a week and I'm fairly frantic. No letter. Was it all too much for you? Have you decided to forego me and lead a sane, uncomplicated life?

To begin where we left off: after the speeding ticket warning, I drove home 45 mph behind a truck all the way. By the time the outskirts of Richland Center hove into view, my teeth were chattering in my head.

Complete silence when I entered the house. "Hello," I said brightly. No answer. I checked on Mark, hung around for awhile, smoked a few cigarettes, waited for someone to say something, and finally went to bed. Jim came in a few minutes later, grabbed some blankets and a pillow, and retired to the living room couch. That couch gets almost as much use as the bed. Next morning he was gone when I got up and came in much later as I was eating lunch and said in a very friendly way, "Want to go bowling this afternoon?" We did, and that was that, except for a few random questions about what I did in Madison and some not so random questions about how the hell I put so many miles on the car. I told him Connor and I had gone to the Dells and thought it wouldn't matter because he could turn the speedometer back. He said he could not, that on vacation last summer he'd unhooked the wires before we left so it wouldn't register, but that it costs ten rotten dollars to have a speedometer set back. The only thing he couldn't understand was how I could buy new shoes, books, overalls for Mark, and stay in Madison on ten dollars. I told him I jumped out of a cake at the Shriner convention for twenty bucks. He didn't doubt it.

The next day I felt as though I'd struggled only to sink deeper into quicksand. Back in Richland Center, no job, very unwilling to steal away to Madison again. Too unnerving.

So yesterday I decided to have it out with him. I appealed to his generosity, his kindness, his ego. I told him I couldn't do the thing alone: surely he realized that we were both unhappy and that to prolong the unhappiness was foolish? Would he help me find a job? He agreed to help. He said it was no use going to Madison on a Saturday, most places were closed, especially the Capitol building. We figured out that a civil service job, while dull, would pay better than most, and that I should take one of their exams. Probably I'll flunk it, but I'll try. Jim is going to work ahead so that he'll be off next Thursday, and I shall take the car and make an all-out effort. I'm determined I won't come back without a job or at least the promise of one.

I know you think I don't really want a job, but I do. I just hate the thought of job-hunting Saturday when we have so little time and it's Mark John's day with his Dad.

It almost seems now as though those two days never happened. They might not have, but for the new shoes and the sand in my hair. Montaigne says memory is sweeter than experience. Perhaps it is, for I now feel that you love me, yet you did nothing to prove that you do. But I found in you a new kindness—a kindness towards human beings in general, compassion I guess you'd call it. Perhaps you simply tossed me in with the rest of mankind, and now I'm mistaking your kindness for more than it was. I don't suppose I'll ever know. Perhaps in twelve more years? If you'd ever really make love to me, perhaps you'd know.

Please write soon. How can I thank you for everything? You were wonderful.

Love, Jennie

*   *   *

Friday, December 10, 1954

Dear Rob,

Jim is out playing poker, the cats are curled under the desk lamp, Mark is tucked into his crib, and all is peace. I've been waiting to write until I had something definite to tell you, but it seems that nothing will be definite for awhile. The last time you heard from me, I was about to go to Madison to look for a job. (Incidently, what were you thinking of to get your letter here on Thursday for my husband to find in the mailbox when he came home early? I had to destroy the precious thing instantly.) To make a long story short, the employment office referred me to WISC-TV which is looking for a continuity and ad writer. I reported and didn't disgrace myself. He told me to go home, write some commercials, send them back and wait. I wrote some great commercials (I thought), sent them back, waited. No news. So finally Joy (my best friend here) drove me to Madison yesterday and I confronted the man. He said the commercials were "damn good," that as soon as the station got organized (it's new) he'd let me know. So there it is: definitely indefinite. I'm going to get that job if it kills me.

I've started a novel! This is rather a left-handed compliment, but you're not in it. It deals with things of "Christmas past," and you're not over with. My pen name is going to be Jennifer McCall. Jennifer McAlister is too much of a mouthful and Jennie too undignified. Jennifer McCall. Nice?

This biding time is hard. Mark was one last Sunday, and Elsie came down and Jim's brother, wife and children came from Madison, and Joy and her husband Chuck came over for manhattans, so it was a shambles. I cooked a big dinner which was the usual dismal failure. I try to keep everything very normal, though I think some people are getting suspicious. They keep asking me why I'm not taking evening art courses this year, why I don't take a scout group, why Jim and I haven't signed up for country club bridge tournament (yes, your Jennie at a country club). I tell them my writing keeps me too busy. This is odd enough, but saves me from darker suspicions.

Joy (tall, slender, pale, red hair) has a good chance at a modeling job in Madison. Her husband is encouraging her—told her to apply and share an apartment with me in Madison while he keeps his job in R.C. Rather an odd marriage, what? Oh, I did so want to tell you in this letter that I was a writer for WISC-TV and sharing an apartment in Madison with Joy. But everything is hanging.

Do write soon, but please not so your letter gets here on a Thursday. Tell me there are better times a comin'.

Love, Jennie

*   *   *

Saturday, January 1, 1955

Dear Jennie,

Home at last on the blessed soil of Iowa. It's the same old story. At first Chicago seemed wildly exciting. Months pass. The faculty turns out to be a bunch of incompetent ninnies whose only mission is to inspire their students to imitate them. The kids reveal themselves as toadying drudges or shallow provincials. The surroundings themselves lose their charm. I can trace this same reaction over the years—first at Roosevelt High, then at Drake, and now here at Chicago.

I am equally disenchanted with the thought of being a teacher, for it's the wildest illusion that I'm going to leave here with an MFA tucked under my arm, set up in a cold attic, and conquer the world. Aunt Marie was right: I'll be a bent old professor in fusty brown, toting my box of dim slides to the classroom and querulously flunking students for not being able to distinguish the ceiling of the Sistine Chapel in Rome from the ceiling of San Giovanni Evangelista in Parma. And you will not even deign to share a garret with me.

My one hope is the Fulbright. It would take me to Italy for a year either as a teacher or a student—I've applied for both. Italy, Rome, Greece have long been my dream, Greece particularly, I think—the white islands in the blue sea. Or perhaps I should just join the Merchant Marines.

Uproarious party at "Ninevah" the night before we all disbanded. Hundreds of people, gallons of booze. Remember my telling you about Staube, the 300-pound baby who paints landscapes on tavern windows and sings Wagner? He was in top form. Found a mop and a pair of deer horns and came charging in à la Wotan bellowing at the top of his lungs to great applause. Never mind that an hour later he was asleep on the floor with his head in a waste basket—he was superb while he lasted. Everyone brought something to drink, everyone sampled everyone else's contribution. As a result, not a few souls felt obliged to spend the night sprawled gently over couches, chairs, beds, and the piano bench.

Have been painting like crazy since I got home—oils, casein, watercolors, anything I can lay my hands on. Feel feverishly inspired.

Have also done a lot of woodcuts. "Kiss of Judas" is my favorite: I'm going to enter it and some oils in a show coming up soon.

What's new? Have you found a job? I must say Jim is being extremely cooperative. In his place I doubt I would help my wife to a job so she could leave me. Or is there good reason behind this unseemly haste? You did say your dinner turned out "for a change." Seriously, I hope you are making progress against the quicksand.

What did you think of the pictures from our October meeting? Or did Jim tear them to shreds before your eyes. You failed to comment.

When will we see each other again? There, I've asked the question twice in a row.

Much love, Rob

*   *   *

Wednesday, March 2, 1955

Dear Rob,

It seems impossible that I haven't written you since before
Christmas.

I was thrilled with the art show clippings. To think that all
these years I doubted your talents. But how can you blame me—I
haven't seen any of your work since those lurid, leggy girls you
used to do in pastels at Delavan and that one blurred clipping from
a Des Moines art show. Please recall that I've been begging for
a painting for years. The interesting part is that had I not known
who did "Kiss of Judas" it still would have been my favorite. The
rhythmic lines are powerful. I am impressed. You're so good and
it's so good that you are.

I now have the odd feeling that I'm writing to a rather superior
being. I must be careful not to make typing or spelling mistakes lest I
be banished forever. What can I possibly write that will interest you?
How you must scorn my inane drivelings!

You ask what is new. Grandmother, for one thing. She is now
permanently confined to a wheelchair, because of Uncle John. Uncle
John is fanatic about polished floors—probably from swabbing the
decks of those sailboats he's so crazy about. Whenever he comes
home, he whips out pail, brush, and polish and goes to work. This
time he waxed the basement stairs. Grandmother is the only person
who ever goes into the basement. Her feet shot out from under on
the first waxed step and she banged all the way to the bottom. The
doctor says it's a miracle she didn't break her neck. She lay there
helpless all day—Uncle John had flown back to Washington and
Aunt Marie was in Milwaukee. Elsie got worried toward suppertime
when the daily phone call failed to materialize and walked up the
hill to investigate.

Uncle John has sent roses from Washington every week since
the disaster, but it's Marie who's going to suffer. She is resigning as
Assistant Dean and Foreign Student advisor at Milwaukee Teachers
College to come home and care for Grandmother.

Speaking of The Witch reminds me, did you know my grandfather died? Peacefully, in his sleep (after a life of Hell) two weeks after Mark was born. He never saw him.

No doubt you are wondering why I'm not in Madison. No word from WISC-TV for one thing. For another, I finally sat down and added up moving expenses. I am deluded to think I can leave on a moment's notice. $100 to move furniture to Madison, $80 down payment on rent, $?? to live on and pay a baby sitter for at least a week until my first paycheck. Jim has kindly offered me some of his New Year's bonus—how he must long to see the last of me—but I won't take it. Oh, Rob, I'll never get out of this! I must be too close to the problem—can't see the exit clearly. If only there weren't Mark—I wouldn't care how I lived for awhile. But I can't be adventurous when a child's concerned—I've got to think and plan.

Have I told you about my big struggle over telling Elsie about the situation? I'd decided against it, then when we were up at Wausau staying with her, Jim left for two days on business. That night Elsie said, "Won't you be glad to have Jim back soon?" I said, "Do you realize that if Jim hadn't been gone I could never have had such a happy evening?" "My poor child," she said, "I know what you've been suffering." We talked until dawn. What a relief—yet she is very unhappy about the situation. I promise that in my next letter I won't utter a word about all this.

Have you heard any more about the Fulbright? What will I do when you're in Italy? Find a postcard in the mailbox if I'm lucky.

I did comment on the pictures. I said I looked disheveled and wan and that the one with my hand to my bosom reminded me of the last five minutes of "Tea and Sympathy." I wish it had been.

When will we see each other again? I'm going to visit Connor in Madison the weekend of March 22 and was going to ask if you could come then. But that would be a low trick to pull on Sarah—I'd never see her the whole time. We might make a charming threesome, but when I see you so seldom, threesomes don't appeal. But perhaps you are not eager for another weekend in Madison after going home sandy and penniless from the last?

Let me know.

Love, Jennie

*   *   *

Monday, April 4, 1955

Dear Jennie,

In exactly two months minus a day I shall be leaving this festering city, my future roped and tied. I've signed on as chairman of the art department at Amarillo College, Amarillo, Texas. Before you go into ecstasies, I had better inform you it's a one man department. Of course, that's my favorite kind, but I know you had instant visions of my commanding hordes.

I leave here June 3 for Des Moines and on June 15 report to Camp Mohawk near Rhinelander as a counselor and waterfront director. Saw the job advertised in our student paper and wrote what must have been a persuasive letter of application to the camp director, a Mr. Sam Miller.

My sister, fortunate girl, will be spending the summer in Hawaii with a current beau—under the watchful eyes of his parents, of course, to keep morality intact.

I have joined a great books club at the urging of a little lass in my lithography class, though I am warned by other students that she is after more than intercourse with my noble mind. Be that as it may, she is one of the few people here who is fun to talk to. Our great books group is ill-assorted and not notable for giant intellects. In fact, it seems most adept at missing an author's point entirely, and at our weekly gatherings I am thrown alternately into fits of righteous anger and abject despair. But at least it makes me read rather carefully, and an occasional pertinent point has been known to stumble forth. Have just finished Gide's "Straight Is the Gate" and find myself identifying uncannily with Jerome. You must get hold of it and see if the story of Alissa and Jerome means anything to you.

Think I will skip Delavan this summer, unless you think you'd like to run out for a few days just for old time's sake. After all, I'll be doing the waterfront bit for eight weeks up at Mohawk. We must see each other. I meant to write sooner, but have been rushing night and day with job applications, interviews, framing canvasses, exhibiting, and finishing a weighty thesis on the Danish painter Edvard Munch. Do you know his work? I could never have made the March 22 weekend, didn't even try. Could you perhaps come to Rhinelander some time? I don't know much about the set-up but I do know that counselors get days off. We could spend one together—just you, me, the lake, and the little campers. Or shall I try to get to Madison? Could we meet in Wausau? Advise.

You will find me resigned to a teacher's life—but not much. I hope you are not becoming resigned to an unhappy marriage. Or have things improved? Don't despair, you will get out—if you want to.

Much love, Rob

Thursday, May 12, 1955

Dear Rob,

Overlook what is going to be an erratic page, for I am using all ten fingers, the fruits of my typing class. You see I'm not lying idle, but preparing for the future. I am also playing the guitar like mad, though I'm less certain how this is going to pave the way for a great career. Segovia inspires me: he makes the guitar sound like a mellow harpsichord.

I sometimes think it's terrible the way small things make me happy. Here I am with Great Troubles on my mind, and am wondrously content picking at six strings. Which brings me to my new theory. All my life I have been looking for The One. When I found Him, our hearts, minds, and souls would meet. He would make Me happy, I would make Him happy. He would complete Me, I would complete Him. Fool, fool to believe in Him so long. I have to find a way to make myself happy and complete. Until I believe in myself, I will believe in no one else.

Think what a huge task it would be to purify one's life, to sluff off all the petty things one does only because they're expected, to get down to the real business. The times and times I've squandered evenings on bridge, not wanting to, yet afraid I'd miss something if I didn't. The mornings and mornings I've idled away over coffee and gossip when I could have been writing. The parties I go to, the games of golf I play. Yet friends are necessary. Life is a riddle. I feel I must decide now whether I want to be a Richland Center social butterfly or try to accomplish something great for once in my life. Have you ever felt this way? But no, you are always accomplishing something.

Jim has been showering me with gifts lately: golf clubs, a set of china, a car coat, an expensive chess set. Perhaps he's trying to bribe me into staying. Either that or he's been winning at poker.

We had a long discussion during which I convinced him that there was nothing he could do about my writing to an old friend (of course he knows). He can't conceive of anything but fornication binding two people together. Or perhaps he hates to admit that anyone shares me in a way he can't. I know he hates you. Sometimes I fear for my safety. But I never want to say goodbye to you. Some summer "that sings in me this while would sing no more."

How fine the Texas job, how dismal that you will be so far away. Texas—the one place I've never wanted to see. At least it's not Italy. Selfish of me, but I was dreading that. Why are you so down on teaching? Are you afraid you won't have time to paint? Banish fears. I have the strongest conviction that you are going to be a great teacher and a great artist.

I'd love to see you. If you're really serious about seeing me why don't you choose the place? Delavan sounds wonderfully nostalgic, but wouldn't it be uncomfortable with your father and Gingy there? They're nice people, but even nice people might be dubious about your "friendship" with a married woman.

I can hardly wait till summer! How many years have I been saying that? Tomorrow is my 22nd birthday. Precious little I've accomplished. But I'm determined that the future will be different.

Love, Jennie

*   *   *

Thursday, June 30, 1955, Camp Mohawk

Dear Jennie,

I am standing by my window (I have no chair, and the cots are too soft to support me and my typewriter), listening to the stirring strains of "Ein Heldenleben," and of course thinking of you.

I have once again studied your portrait and rather like it now. Without you here in person it is quite easy to convince myself that I have captured an exact likeness.

I arrived in Rhinelander at 9:30 and in camp at 10:30, having become lost in the maze of little roads around the place. I'm sure you recall that when I took the wheel that fatal day in Milwaukee we immediately became lost. Nothing has changed. That is why I wanted to leave earlier than later. The camp director was insultingly glad to see me and his car back safely.

Naturally I would love to read the first chapters of your novel. It could be that you write better than me. I would also really like to see some of your serious drawings. It could be that you draw better than me. Naturally I would never admit either circumstance—I would just go off and take poison. I hope you realize I was not playing my most brilliant chess game. Had I been in top form it would have taken you at least another 10 minutes to checkmate me.

Thank your mother for me. It was good seeing her again after all these years. She is a most charming lady. Give Mark a big hug and don't let him eat Cheerios all day.

That damned loudspeaker is going to go off and announce some ghastly activity at any moment—

I miss you. I hated to leave. It was all I could do to tear myself away from the wine, your open kimona, and your lovely room.

Rob

*　　*　　*

Thursday, July 15, 1955

Dear Rob,

Richland Center again. Oh god.
You probably realized I was very happy to see you. It was idyllic—the rainy day, the moon at night. The wine. The fire. Wouldn't it be heavenly to spend days just listening to all the music we love? To have days and days to talk over all the things we care and wonder about, and to read favorite books aloud that we've always wanted to share.

I've just finished "Stright Is the Gate." It haunts me. You remind me in so many ways of Jerome. But I can't compare myself to Alissa. Alissa denied herself to Jerome because she wanted to give him to God. I don't agree that when two people love each other they must love God—or art or spirit or whatever you want to call it—less. Surely God (whatever that is) meant us to know human love and only finally divine love. I've also read Maurois' "Ariel" on your recommendation. Do you like Shelley or Byron better? Do you agree with Shelley—atheism, free love, revolution? You'll know which poet I prefer.

My novel is at the seventh chapter. I've vowed not to show it to anyone and so far have not, but if I ever do let someone besides a publisher read it, it will be you. But advise me: do you prefer novels written in the first person or third? I know what you'll say—it all depends. I'm writing in the first person, but am having a devil of a time deciding whether I should be there. I feel right in first person and I like the camera view I get, but it's so limited. Nothing can go on that the narrator doesn't know about. I also wonder whether the "I" doesn't get rather tiring, especially in a long book. Please shed a ray of light.

We spent a weekend in Milwaukee recently, celebrating Jim's brother's birthday. He couldn't understand why I wanted to drive around the city, but I said I was nostalgic for Downer days. I noted with tenderness all the little spots: Riverside Theatre, dear old Bradford Beach, dear old Marietta House, Estabrook Park. Do you remember the big stone mansion by the lake (where the toilet seat was up), near the path that led down to a narrow and treacherous strip of beach? We took pictures there once and I had long hair and was wearing a paisley skirt and an off-the-shoulder white blouse (in fact I remember my whole wardrobe from those days in bright detail, but shall abstain). The path is no more, houses crowd right down to the lake, and there's a big sign PRIVATE PROPERTY KEEP OUT.

I hesitated, but decided not to call Donald. He was never very good over a phone (though he used the instrument frequently) and frankly, I didn't know what to say. Maybe we could have met on the beach—he with his niece and me with Mark John. What a hangin' reunion that would have been. We could have counted our grey hairs.

Do write to your exiled

Jenny

*   *   *

Saturday, July 30, 1955, Camp Mohawk

Dear Jennie,

A nice note from your mother which I will try to answer after this as I hope to spend part of next Friday with her in Wausau. I'm looking forward to an exceptionally pleasant day off.

My cabin has won best cabin award three times in the last four days. You see what trifles make me happy in this wilderness. Have been on one overnight and anticipate another shortly. Can relax a bit on these sylvan retreats, but fail to get much of a charge from sleeping on the hard ground in a bag filled with pine needles, sand, acorns, and probably a beastie or two. Man has labored 5000 years to get away from this sort of thing.

Have bought some glorious records. The Rhinelander Disc Shop was having a big sale of classical labels that evidently have not been moving too quickly with the tourist trade. Picked up Schonberg's Verklarte Nacht, the Daphnis and Chloe suites, Also Sprach Zarathustra, Beethoven's Eighth, Mendelssohn's Fourth, the German Requiem and excerpts from Der Rosenkavalier. I play my taddies to sleep with the German Requiem, and have had surprisingly few complaints. Have made, in fact, one rabid convert—the son of a wealthy Wisconsin sausage maker. I happened to be standing nearby said son and father on Parents Day last week when father asked what little present his boy might like to welcome him home after camp. He beamingly waited for Sonny to order a motorcycle, speedboat, or saddle horse. "The record of Schonberg's Verklarte Nacht, please," lisped Dan winningly. The expression on Pater's face when he finally figured out what Filius was talking about defies description.

The few spare, untroubled moments I wrest out of the day I spend with Thomas Mann's Confessions of Felix Krull. Perfect summer reading—the substance is all there but it is light and easy-going, a far cry from The Magic Mountain. About point of view. Of course, "it all depends." Some narratives are better told from one person's view, some from all-seeing omniscience. It depends on the scope you wish to achieve. Personally I prefer third person. Mann's books, for example, or Flaubert, Lewis or Dreiser. I like the distance and the narrator's ability to get into all the characters' minds. But with seven chapters written I would hesitate to change the whole thing. Why not let me read it?

A pity you didn't call Donald. He would have been delirious with joy. He told me recently in a letter that "those years" were the best part of his life and that he didn't expect anything better from the future. I told him not to be an idiot.

Now, can you possibly meet me in Madison August 16? Camp ends the 15th, but it will take me a day to get my gear together and get down there. Unless you think, of course, that twice in one summer is too much . . .

Let me hear.

Love, Rob

* * *

Friday, August 5, 1955

Dear Rob,

I do not think twice in one summer is too much, so I will come to Madison. Aurore Dudevant and I, both flying about the countryside—she to political rallies, I to you.

I shall meet you at the Loraine Hotel between ten and eleven Saturday morning. Will that be all right? I hope no next-door neighbors are rendezvousing at the same spot. I find my situation growing intolerable, and the desire to know something apart from the sphere of my sorrow (to borrow Shelley) growing stronger every day. At the same time I realize it's up to me to break the sphere.

Today two friends and I are throwing a big lunch and card party at the Country Club. For weeks we've been planning what we will serve—shrimp bisque over rice, salad, and apple pie. I have an apple pie cooling in the kitchen. I mock how thoroughly I play Mrs. Jim.

Till Saturday then.

Love, Jennie

* * *

Friday, August 19, 1955

Dear Rob,

By slim threads do our fortunes hang. This morning I walked into Junie Wilson's meat market (like a moth to flame was I drawn). Junie's ruddy face rose behind the counter.

"Morning, Jennie. Say, isn't it a small world. My brother Sam paid a visit over the weekend and of all things he knows a friend of yours."

My heart stopped.

"Darndest thing. My brother's the caretaker at a camp near Rhinelander and knows this friend of yours who's waterfront director this summer. Why he even drove the guy to Madison a few days ago. Said that this Rob Falkner mentioned he had friends in Richland Center—the Jim Brandts. 'No!' says my brother. 'I was born and raised in Richland Center. I bet they know my brother Junie. Must tell him.' Seems this Falkner is coming to Richland Center to see you. Has he?"

"No," says I faintly, "haven't heard from him."

"You know, I was figuring to tell Jim about it when I saw him yesterday, but it clean slipped my mind."

"Pity he didn't show up," I murmur. "Old, old friend."

With leaden heart I paid for my pork chops at the checkout counter, then came back.

"Junie," I says, "please don't mention this to Jim."

He looks surprised. "O.k., Jennie, if you don't want me to."

"Rob's an old childhood friend, but Jim—you know . . ."

Junie ponders this.

"Must be why the guy didn't show up in Richland Center after all. Too bad in a way."

And then the words I wanted to hear: "Don't worry, this is just between you and I."

So by fortune's grace, Sam Wilson thought you were innocently coming to Richland Center, and Junie forgot to mention it to Jim. Saved.

After I left you last Sunday I went to Connor's, hoping that somehow she could staunch the pain I felt at saying goodbye to you again.

There are four people in the world I can run to for comfort—Elsie, Connor, Joy, and now you.

Connor was reading Japanese poetry and eating lamb chops. I dropped onto the couch, exhausted. She put away the poetry and put "Carmina Burana" on the record player. The stately melodies of the wandering medieval students lulled me. "Oh, fortuna," they sang, "variable as the moon." "Go to sleep, Jennie," said Sarah. "I'm going to feed Ellen's pigeons. She's teaching them to distinguish pink from white." I did not wonder but fell instantly asleep.

When I crept into the house at six, Jim would not speak to me. Who can blame him. I went to bed and dreamed, half sleeping, half awake, hoping that morning would never come.

Thank you for giving me more than I asked for, more than I expected. You were honest with me and have given me the courage to be honest with myself. I feel better loved and cherished than before. I hope you felt some of the love I feel for you, so that if you want it you can take it, if you need it, it is there.

Jennie

* * *

Sunday, September 12, 1955

I have waited long and late for a letter. No mail ever comes to the house any more. If you've written, then Jim has intercepted the letters. If you haven't, I'm even more distressed.

Jim knows about Madison—not from Junie but from some completely unexpected source. When he returned he went for me, bouncing me like a basketball off our bedroom walls. If Mark hadn't started crying, I don't know what might have happened.

It doesn't matter: nothing could ruin our relationship further. I am going to Wausau and staying there until I find a job.

When you write—if you write—please send the letter in an envelope addressed to Mrs. Joy Le Mieux, 420 1/2 North Fairmont Street, Richland Center.

I'll let you know when I leave.

Jennie

*   *   *

Friday, September 16, 1955

Dear Jennie,

Your letter of the 12th reached me only this afternoon. Did you get my last one, written over a week ago and addressed to 571 Fairmont? If Jim has it, he won't be happy with you.

I cannot be sorry that the thing between you and Jim has finally come to a head, and that you are being compelled to take a stand. If the situation is as intolerable—and as physically dangerous—as you claim, an end is inevitable. To my thinking, the sooner the better.

With people like Connor, Joy and your mother about, I don't think you can complain about being alone, though throngs of suitors may not be panting to snatch up the prize as soon as Jim fades. I know this sounds cold and cruel, but it's not meant to be. I know how you must feel at this point, but if you can't live with him, why persist?

How are you? Where are you? Where is Mark John? Have you been put out, as threatened, or do things still go on as before?

Lean on my shoulder too, Jennie. It is not as hard as it may seem at times. And what is it Alissa keeps telling Jerome: "I could not be closer to you now if we were in the same room touching one another's hands." That book fills me with frustration. I wonder why.

Rob

Call it morbid curiosity (and you will), but who was the unexpected source that let Jim know about Madison? I thought we were totally unnoticed by anyone save the music librarian, so pleased that someone wanted to listen to Wagner at last.

*　　*　　*

Monday, September 26, 1955

Dear Rob,

Thank you for writing in care of Joy. It was so wonderful to hear from you at last. I don't know how many letters you've written, but they undoubtedly fell into Jim's hands—I can think of no other explanation.

Jim chose to be evasive about where he'd heard that I'd been in Madison with you. He said that a gas station attendant in RC asked him how he'd enjoyed the weekend in Madison and seeing his old friend again. This sounds most unlikely, though coincidences do happen. I hate to believe that Junie Wilson broke his word.

I am not, as you see, in Wausau. I've been working on my novel and little else. Between typewriter sessions I plan my escape. I want to get together about $300, find an apartment in Madison, then have a month with money to live on while I find a job, an apartment mate, and a nursery or sitter for Mark. I tried to do all this last spring by running to and from Richland Center. I had a job, but no apartment. I had a nursery for Mark, but no job. I had a roommate, but no car. Now I have a car (Jim has given me the second-hand convertible) and I think my new plan may work.

You have no doubt written all about Amarillo College in your lost letters. I hate to make you describe it all over again, but I must know what it's like and whether you're enjoying your new world. They undoubtedly look upon you as some young genius. How I would love to fly away to Texas, but I'm afraid I could not brave all the uncertanties—not the least of which is the fear you would turn me from your door.

Perhaps you could come to Madison during the Christmas holidays. I would be working, but if you came on a weekend we could have two days together. Oh, please come.

Thank you for Alissa's words to Jerome. They could not have meant more to him than they did to me.

Love, Jennie

* * *

Wednesday, September 28, 1955

Dear Jennie,

So much has happened since I last wrote that I don't know where to begin; but first, has anything happened to you? Have you left? Have you found a job? Is Jim speaking to you? I shall continue to write under cover to Joy, though I feel guilty of the darkest intrigue. And poor Joy—how frustrating to get and not get letters, so to speak.

I drove to Amarillo in my own car. Yes, at last, a car. Nothing splashy, but adequate. A 1955 Ford, green. Arrived barely in time to make it to the faculty breakfast Thursday morning. Stumbled into the room bleary-eyed from much driving and suffering from a god-awful sinus infection that had me stone deaf, runny nosed, and twitchy faced: hardly the burning young genius.

Anyway, here I am, chairman of the Art Department, and one-man department or not, I'm just beginning to realize the responsibility involved. The more I see of the school, the more impressed I am. Lavish supplies and equipment. Uniformly conservative modern architecture, beautifully kept grounds. I have a spacious private office tucked away in a corner of the Creative Arts building overlooking the campus. There's an immense empty room adjoining the office which I plan to convert into a studio if the administration doesn't complain.

I don't know the faculty well enough yet to pass judgment, but already I can pick out the ones I'm going to like, dislike, and ignore. I appear at least ten years younger than any of them, and am fast getting weary of being mistaken for a student or somebody's son. In fact, the college librarian checked my selection of books today (Maurois' Life of Proust and Gide's The Immoralist).

"Are these for your English class, young 'un?"

"No, for my own pleasure."

"Oh, how splendid you're starting to read good books so young."

This is all doubly amusing because I have never felt older nor worked harder. I'm trying desperately to get the Art Department and my classes into shape while at the same time keeping up with endless faculty meetings. This week we advise and register students. I'm doing my best to steer all counselees away from Hobbies and Crafts, the one course I don't give a damn about teaching.

I've found a decent apartment. Good quarters at a reasonable price are hard to come by in Amarillo, but this place is livable though cramped. The neighborhood is middle-class, close to college, and since I'm in a garage I can blast with the hi-fi and disturb no one. My landlady is a shrewd old devil and a formidable talker. Unless I have an hour or two to spare I must avoid her sight. By the way, the address is 211 Ong Street (sounds like a Chinese laundry, doesn't it). But write me at the college since I have a dark suspicion that I'll be spending most of my time there.

Are you still planning to run away to Amarillo? I think not, but you are welcome on my doorstep. It has been a long time between letters, but I think of you often and worry about you too. I have your picture—the smiling-faced one—pinned up on my cluttered bulletin board so that when school becomes too tiresome or I become too lonely I can wink over at you and be cheered. Is that magnificent hair still long, I hope?

Things should settle down here, and I'll try to write often. Please do the same.

As ever, Rob

*   *   *

Wednesday, October 5, 1955

Dear Rob,

What a joyous afternoon! I just bought ten record albums for 59 cents a piece. Of course, they're 78's, but still.

I know you can't wait to hear what they are: Strauss—Don Juan, Berlioz—Symphonie Fantastique, Mozart—Piano Concerto 21, Wagner-Die Walküre, Brahms—Double Concerto, Beethoven—Symphonies 4 and 6, Prokofiev—Alexander Nevsky, Hayden—Quartets, and Wagner—Die Meistersinger (excerpts).

I carried them home in ecstasy and Jim said, "You are not playing the phonograph, I am watching television."

"All night?"

"All night."

This is always the way it is. I hate, hate, hate him.

(Lord, he's just come in, hiding this.)

Monday morning—1 a.m. I'm taking silly pills that keep me wide awake. Must write, must do something.

I've managed to scrape together $300 from various sources. I'm now seriously considering San Francisco as my goal. Everyone who's been there gives it rave notices. I've given up Madison for two reasons: my dear Connor graduated this summer and is leaving this Tuesday for Europe for two years, and my associations with Madison (apart from our meetings there) are quite unpleasant.

I have thought of Amarillo, much as the thought of hot, dusty plains repels me, but somehow I feel that you'd think I was there to—well, to keep an eye on you, press you, spoil your new adventure. I might too, not being a mouse content with small crumbs.

But San Francisco—all the best rolled into one: the sophistication of New York, the beauty of Washington, the antiquity of Boston—and ocean, mountains, forests all within easy reach. And many colleges in the area, all dying for a brilliant young art instructor. I just know it must by my city—and yours.

I sing "Oh, Fortuna" as I plod through my chores, feeling superior to other housewives who, I am sure, do not chant Latin while they work. "Oh, Fortuna"—flip goes the dust mop, "Velut luna"—swish goes the scrub water, "Statu variabilis"—BANG go the dishes in the pan.

I wonder if this period of doubt and indecision will ever end. I feel it is about to, somehow. It terrifies me to realize I can do almost anything with my life. It scares me too to realize how few chances I'll take because I'm afraid. But my fear is slowly dissolving. If I could only dispell it completely I might almost be reborn.

I'm tired at last and think I can sleep. Please continue sending letters to Joy until further notice. How I wish I could fall asleep and wake up in your apartment, like Catherine flung down onto Wuthering Heights in her dream.

To bed.

Love, Jennie

*   *   *

Monday, October 17, 1955

Dear Jennie,

Your last letter was in so much more cheerful vein that I too was cheered. It arrived when my spirits were particularly subdued. I had just returned from a Religious Week assembly: all week Amarillo College has been given over to the Christian crusade. I have tried to put myself into a state of suspended animation, but I can't help listening and observing, and can only conclude that this college is rife with obsolete elements that have no business in higher education.

Your records sound like quite a bargain, though running to the machine every three minutes to flip a 78 would soon have me unnerved and irritable. Has Jim let you play them yet? Glad you are developing a taste for Wagner. My complete Gotterdamerung has arrived, but I've only had time to listen to the first three sides. Flagstad's voice is not what it was—she slides into her high notes with piercing shrieks—but is still beautiful within a limited range.

I have finished The Immoralist and like it very much, even better perhaps than Straight Is the Gate. Don't want to disturb you, but I fear I'm closer to Michael than Jerome. I become more disillusioned and indolent every moment. Have taken to lounging in my office eating Nestle Crunch Bars and drinking Dr. Peppers for hours on end while untouched work piles up around my neck and my empty easel stares reproachfully in the face. Perhaps this trough of idleness is a reaction finally against last year. I never worked so hard as I did that final semester. Thought many times I'd never pull it through.

For god's sake, if you're going to leave, leave! Though one thing bothers me—Mark John. You could hardly take him to San Francisco, could you? You both would wind up in a Chinese opium den, and I would stumble across you quite by accident years from now, like Larry Darrell finding Sophie in The Razor's Edge. You would gaze at me from vacant eyes and silently resume your pipe. Seriously, Jennie, I think it's mad for you to rush off to a city you don't know, where you have no friends nor certainty of a job.

If you were to fall asleep and wake up transplanted to my apartment it would be with a cry of horror rather than delight. The place is the size of a roomy pill-box; and though I wouldn't mind cramped quarters if they were romantically located in a garret or a secret room, the charm of a garage on Ong Street escapes me. I must admit your arrival in Amarillo would rather stagger me, but we could throw a couple of cushions on the floor for a bed and you could set up housekeeping with a hot plate. Of course, you would have to hide out from my landlady during the day. It would be like playing Phantom of the Opera.

How is your novel coming?

Are you going to leave or aren't you?

Love, Rob

* * *

Tuesday, November 1, 1955

Dear Rob,

Much has happened since I last wrote. I've abandoned thoughts of Madison, Milwaukee, Amarillo and San Francisco—all because of Aunt Marie.

I told Elsie never to tell her about my situation, but since Elsie has never kept a secret in her life, my request was less than useless. About three weeks ago Aunt Marie descended upon Richland Center. We had the longest talk we've ever had in my life. She said, to be brief, that if I would "prove myself" by leaving, getting a job and saving some money, she would help finance college for me next year. She's convinced I must go back to school. I suppose I agree.

The best place for me to work, she thinks, is Wausau. My mother would move to a larger apartment and I would live with her, sharing rent and food. Oh, I don't want to go back there! Divorced, defeated, all my friends long gone or smugly married. But I thought and thought, and I guess it's best. For awhile.

So it's been decided and I feel something like calm for the first time in two years. I don't look forward to taking Mark away from Jim. It will be ghastly. The only thing that comforts me is the fact that if I left Mark with him it would be twice as ghastly. He knows Mark from five p.m. to eight p.m., I know him all day. I would never give him up.

I think the future looks fairly bright. Incurable optimist, I know. Jim is negative and always has been. "You'll never be happy," he mutters darkly. Oh yes, I will, Jim. Not understanding me in the least, you don't know what makes me happy, but I can be.

It's a warm, grey November day, much like the day two and a half years ago I realized I was going to have a baby. I thought then that my life was over—in fact (I've never told you this) I contemplated ending it. I didn't know how, but thought I'd swim from the Union pier until I couldn't anymore—or lock myself in Jim's garage with the motor running. But I've been given another chance. Incredible, how we're always being given another chance.

I haven't said this very well. Perhaps you can guess how I feel.

You'd better continue to write through Joy.

Love, Jennie

P.S. What do you mean you're more like Michael than Jerome? Michael was an insufferable egotist who preferred Arab boys to his wife!

*   *   *

Tuesday, November 15, 1955

Dear Jennie,

Hurrah! What good news. I've always had a lurking suspicion that Marie would save the day, and I'm relieved beyond words that you're not bolting for San Francisco. When do you leave for Wausau? Is Jim resigned? Poor little Mark, caught in the midst of all this. I suppose he's too young to realize much.

The novelty of Amarillo College is wearing off and the drudgery of it all emerging. I need a change of scene about every six weeks to keep me happy, I guess. It's an awful way to be, but that's about all I can take before things start to fray. The students are lazy as hell but pretty good. The faculty is grim: withered old maids and big cowlike men who sit around telling dirty jokes with much slapping of thighs, winking of eyes, and slobbering of mouths. I retire to my office, apply for fellowships, and drown myself in Royal Crown Colas.

Strange to say, however, I seem to have created a bit of a stir here. The photography people are doing a movie starring me and the Art Department. Then the students have organized into a group they call Bizarre. I'm afraid it will prove just that, but the fact that the students have organized at all is a first is the history of the school, and the administration is impressed. I am preparing canvasses for an exhibit. The local newspaper is doing an article about me: if it's long and exciting I'll send you a copy. The sweetest little thing interviewed me—about four feet tall with a pony tail five feet long and glasses two inches thick. Something tells me she'll produce quite a story.

Had a mad excursion the other weekend. Drove up to Colorado Springs with Fritz Dard (local art dealer and personality), Gilda Dettmer (an incredibly gorgeous fiftyish creature who owns the Panhandle), and May Pinton (a local china painter who is hot after Fritz'a body while he, alas, chases pretty boys). They went to see artists; I went to see Pike's Peak, but found it smothered in blankets of fog, so went and saw artists too. Fell in with the weirdest crew of mystics, visionaries, and yogis. We called on a hermit sculptor named Sylvester Gladtree, who foruntately was in the mood to let us invade his sanctuary. He is steeped in the lore of Eastern mysteries, practices yogi and god knows what else. His walls were covered with paintings of savage

Oriental women with huge breasts and gilded nipples staring down from all sides. Grotesque, writhing pieces of sculpture everywhere. Little old Sylvester, however, seemed happy enough to see us, and led us from creation to creation, discussing literature, art, politics, and sex in a very unmystical way. Somehow I seem to attract strange people, unholy places.

Donald writes that his father has died. Said it's a blessing as the old man was eaten up with cancer. That leaves Donald to take over the family's fortunes at the tender age of 22. Don't think he'll be able to manage it. Don't think his father ever thought he could. Donald once told me (unnecessarily) that he was the disappointment of his father's life. Don't think fathers should rely on sons. Made that crystal clear to mine long ago. The Lindsay family address, in case you wish to extend condolences, is 3929 Shoreline Drive.

I have not forgotten you. I still worship you from afar and hope you'll let me know quickly what is transpiring in Richland Center and Wausau.

Love, Rob

*   *   *

Thursday, November 17, 1955

Dear Rob,

I've put my hair up and gone to work. The job is receptionist, typist (smirk not, I've improved), proofreader and odd job girl at the Marathon Press, a small, new, informal and pleasant printing company. It's run by a large, middle-aged, informal and pleasant man. Have an idea I could get "credits," but one Monty in a lifetime is enough for me. There is a machine with tolerable coffee, donuts at 10 a.m., and the pay is pretty good. I also get Saturdays off—that's what finally sold me.

Obviously I'm in Wausau. Elsie moved, and the three of us are living in a spacious six room apartment that occupies the whole first floor of a large Victorian house. There's a yard for Mark with trees, a fence and a swing set. There are two living rooms, one with an old—fashioned tile fireplace. The dining room is paneled in dark wood, with a cross-beamed ceiling, diamond window panes and velvet covered window seats. When the sun shines the diamond panes fling rainbows across the room.

Mother's current beau Shep (a scientist, inventor, farmer, and nudist) drove down to Richland Center to get my things with his trailer. Picture this. Across the street from our apartment is a grocery store. All Richland Center shops there on Saturday. It was Saturday. It took two hours to load my things. For two full hours the store-front was jammed with faces. Friends drove by in cars, waving or stopping to offer to help. Enemies rode by, jeering openly. Phones rang. Jim was conveniently out of it all in Madison. Joy was right there helping. We tottered out with the dishes. Shep didn't like the way they were packed, so there were Joy and I taking out every damn dish and packing all over again under the eyes of the multitude. At the last moment Shep and I quarreled over a pail of soaking diapers. He said no self-respecting woman would leave behind a pail of dirty diapers. I said any father with self-respect would not have let a diaper pail sit there for two bloody weeks. He said it was my responsibility. I said it wasn't. He said he was not leaving until I washed them. I I'd drive his trailer back to Wausau myself. We left in bitter silence. Yet I feel I've done my civic duty toward Richland Center. Through a long, dull winter, they will have something to talk about.

I have what I pray is a competent baby sitter for Mark. My worry is that she weighs 270 pounds. I pay her extra to come to our house (hate the idea of taking Mark to someone's else's home), but I think she's double-crossing me. Several times I've got home from work to find her huffing and purple—for all the world as though she's just toiled the two blocks up the hill from her house. I've tried to get Mark to rat on her, so far no luck.

I still write, but now at snatched moments—locked behind doors while Elsie's drama group emotes in the adjacent room; during Captain Kangaroo while Mark is quiet. If Mr. Greenjeans creeps into the story I won't be surprised. Having a devil of a time with punctuation. Do you put thoughts in quotes? E.g. Ellen thought, "I can't bear this." And what do you use before a quotation—a comma or a colon? Ellen thought: "I can't bear this." Right?

There's a young man living upstairs who reminds me of you. I went up one day and he was lounging in a chair stroking a Siamese. He is languid, dark, and slender. His voice also has a slight husky rasp like yours. He's quiet too (you keep telling me you are). But of course there's no substitute for the genuine article.

If you're going to be lazy and decadent, can't you manage something more exotic than Nestle bars and Royal Crown cola? And why are you bored and indolent at all? Do you want me to become a famous novelist before you become a famous artist? Of course you don't. Think of me rattling away at the typewriter, nearer every moment to fame and fortune, while you laze away the hours. But of course you aren't really indolent at all—that's just a pose—the Art Department is obviously humming. Do send the article.

Poor Donald, the burden of empire on his shoulders!

Well, darling, I have escaped. No, I didn't think there would be suitors hovering around to pick up the prize. But if there isn't one beloved person who now feels a little of my relief and sense of freedom, some of the triumph will be spoiled.

Can't you come to Wausau for Christmas?

Love, Jennie

*   *   *

Friday, January 6, 1956

Dear Jennie,

A relaxed Christmas in Des Moines, and a white one too. But the trip back to Amarillo was a nightmare—500 miles of ice, sleet, and snow. I often feared I wouldn't make it. The black Persian kitten I acquired over the holidays spent most of the miles sitting on my left shoulder gazing complacently out the window.

I have returned to Amarillo feeling very much like painting and finding not a moment to do it. The end of semester rush is here: the dismal process of grading papers, making out final exams, and turning in piles of useless records to the dean. Teaching might be bearable if all this stuff weren't part of it.

I'm enclosing a sample of some recent publicity. The big play I got in the papers was due mainly to the good offices of the local Amusement Editor (art is amusement in Amarillo), who came to the opening of my show and was impressed. Her review is pretty nonsensical, but it did bring throngs of people to see my paintings. Despite this I didn't sell a great deal, and I expect that many of those who are still talking excitedly of buying will fail to come through with the cold cash. It is so depressing—here I am, a great artist but with no name, so that virtually nobody will buy. Someday I'm going to have an enormous bonfire.

Between grading exams I'm reading the Journals of Andre Gide. Once I find an author I have to search out everything he wrote before I turn to something else. The Journals are sometimes dull, sometimes beautiful, sometimes startling: "I am a pederast." I didn't know this—perhaps you did?

I have managed to move. No longer do I suffocate between the four walls of a garage. Another fellow and myself have rented a spacious house, and my bedroom is now larger than my former apartment. We each have a private bath, there is a huge living and dining room, wall to wall carpets, and a large kitchen (not yet used). Two davenports, an organ, a T.V. (also not yet used), two hi-fi's, a tape recorder, etc. etc. I now have a place to put you, should you ever fly to Amarillo.

Your mother is dating a nudist? I hope Grandmother and Marie don't know. Come to think of it, I hope the rest of Wausau doesn't known either, though I myself find the idea perfectly enchanting.

How about starting to save your money for Europe next September? We've talked about it for years—let's really go. I don't want to go in summer when it's overrun with American tourists and as European as Coney Island. Then too, another summer at Mohawk will give me another $500 to use abroad. I will try to get a leave of absence from the college. Much will depend on whether my predecessor here finishes his degree and returns.

I've just noticed, with a shock, that your last letter was postmarked months ago (slight exaggeration). God knows what has happened to you in the interim.

Save for Europe. Write for fame and fortune. And never trust quiet young men who stroke Siamese cats. They are the devil's own.

Love, Rob

Yes, thoughts are put in quotes: Rob thought, "Is Jennie happy with her new life?" Rob also thought, "Colons, commas—it's all the same. One for long, formal thoughts, the other for shorter, informal musings."

*   *   *

Tuesday, January 17, 1956

Dear Rob,

Yes, something did happen in the "interim"—I almost died waiting for a letter. I try to bear the silences calmly, but I can't. While you made merry in Des Moines and sapped up Royal Crown colas, my novel went awry, I snapped at my child, and spent hours stubbing out cigarette butts and cursing you. Please do not torture me so again. I went over my letter mentally a hundred times wondering what I could have said to offend you. Wicked lad, to cause me such pain.

How can I save money for Europe next September when I promised my aunt that I'd salt away my shekels for school? Even if I could afford it, it's pretty much unheard of for a single male and female to travel together sharing a bed, isn't it? It seems that bad ends always come to people who do, at least to females who do. Shall we defy convention? Besides, what am I to do with Mark? Still, the very thought of going abroad with you stirs me to blissful frenzy.

Sheperd Schlegel, my mother's current flame, is only a part-time nudist, indulging chiefly when he's out hoeing his acres in the summertime. My mother dropped in on him last summer with a couple of women friends. He wasn't about the house, so they wandered into the fields. Saw a hand waving, saw vegetation parting, saw Shep striding towards them clad only in suntan. The cowards all fled shrieking.

I'm about to commence divorce proceedings. My lawyer is Mr. Berger, my old Sunday school teacher. The first thing he said was, "Well, Jennie, if you had gone to Sunday School more often this never would have happened." I wanted to fire him on the spot. He can't figure out grounds for the divorce. When I told him Jim almost killed me one night, he said, "But how can you blame him when you just came home from seeing another man?" He insists there must be Another Man and in his heart believes that Jim should be getting the divorce, not me. I tell him wearily that Jim and I were simply incompatible, but that's not grounds in Wisconsin. Jim's got to be an adulterer or something filthy. Don't know how it will all end.

I had such a vivid dream about you that when I woke I sat up and wrote it down before I forgot:

You have invited me to spend Christmas in Des Moines. I am going to fly a plane there myself, though I don't know how. I get in, pull back the stick and SENSATION the plane rises. I land in Des Moines. You are there. You whisk me off immediately to a dinner party. All the people there turn out to be my friends.

You are shy and embarrassed. I make bright chatter to put you at ease, and get out sheets of drawing paper. We draw during dinner, forgetting the others.

We are alone on a couch. We notice a figure in the shadows studying books on a shelf. He steps out of the shadows. SENSATION. It is Donald Lindsay. It is Jim. He sits down on the couch and studies you carefully. I desperately try to make conversation. You lie down on the floor and pout. I turn to smile at you and find you have turned into a baby. This embarrasses me. Jim hasn't noticed. I try to distract him so he won't look down at the baby on the floor. In spite of my strenuous efforts he looks.

You are not there. I feel a hand on my shoulder. It is you. You have sheets of drawing paper in your hand. You smile, you say Come, we must draw together. My heart beats fast with joy. You lead the way into a dark room, you disappear behind the door. I follow. The room is empty. I hear a baby crying far away.

Know any dream analysts?

Since I'm doing the narrative bit, I think I'll copy out for you the paragraph of my novel I've just written. If I'm ever going to unveil my prose I have to start somewhere.

Her room was monastic in its simplicity. As if to atone for her sensual indulgence, Ellen denied herself ordinary comforts. She chose the hardest, narrowest bed in the house. As autumn turned to winter, she left the windows of her third floor room wide open. She ate little, but in a small hamper near her desk kept apples, crackers, and raisins. Though often hungry, she seldom touched them. In performing these rituals of self-abnegation, she hoped to obliterate the acts of sexual indulgence she committed. She did not realize that denial only exaggerated indulgence, and mocked it relentlessly.

Tell me:

do you

think

I'll

ever

be

a

SUCCESS?

Don't think I want to know. Can you come up with a title? Something good, like Straight Is the Gate.

Marc is banging his highchair to be fed.

Please, not another month. Please, please.

Love, Jennie

*　　*　　*

Thursday, February 2, 1956

Wicked girl, evil mind!
I'm hurt and shocked at your attitude toward our European fling.

Does the opinion of the narrow-minded, sterile, vapid throngs so trouble you, a free spirit? You forsake the great adventure for fear of defying convention? Besides, we two are so inconspicuous and unimportant that our idyll will hardly wag many tongues. And the "bad end" is just your Puritan conscience. I rather think this sort of thing usually ends quite well . . .

Of course, if you really object to being alone, I could bring along any number of silly students and dull faculty who are clamoring to accompany me. If it would mean getting your company I'd be glad to band together the whole motley crew. Or we could arrange to become acquainted on shipboard, two strangers meeting by chance on the rolling sea. I would offer to light your cigarette by the light of the voodoo moon, your eyes would lift to mine . . . . And you cast it all aside!

I shouldn't say this—you will kill me, yourself, or both of us—but I think your dream makes better reading than the novel excerpt. Why not publish Dreams By Jennie McAllister and I will lavishly illustrate it. My dreams are not half so good. The other night I dreamed that my design class gave me one of the students as a present—unfortunately a sullen creature named Linda. The next scene was my apartment. I was trying to sleep and keep an eye on Linda at the same time. She kept trying to crawl into bed and I kept kicking her out and silently wondering why my design students had such bad taste. No one spoke a word. Analyze that if you dare.

Seriously, your little paragraph is not at all bad. Too many heavy words in the last two sentences: cut the "self-denials" and the "self-abnegations" by half. At least your prose is not rife with underlinings and exclamations as I feared. If I had a dollar all these years for every word you ____ or !! I could retire tomorrow. How can I suggest a title when I don't know what the book is about? Of course, that seldom bothers a publisher. How about Raised Is the Drawbridge? Wide Is the Moat? Barren Is My Boudoir? Busy Is My Bed? Though I hope the latter is not true, it would sell a million copies.

My new place is quite comfortable, and if only I derived some pleasure from cooking I could be happy, but the kitchen is loathsome to me, and I am driven by hunger and desperation to eat out more often than, for the sake of economy, I should. I am trying to get the home economics teacher to assign her girls "supper for Rob Falkner" as homework, but she says they are undoubtedly worse cooks than I. I suspect she believes my hunger is of the flesh rather than the stomach.

How is Mark John? Do be careful of him and have pillow fights now and then. When does the divorce ordeal take place?

Forgive me for having been so wretchedly slow in answering your letters. I punish myself more than I do you by these long delays, as it makes the time between letters from Wausau unbearably long. Please be kind, merciful, answer soon, and say yes to our European fling.

Love, Rob

P.S. 23 years old in four days. Senility in seven years.

*   *   *

Friday, February 17, 1956

Dear Rob,

The other night for the first time I began to think of going to Europe seriously. Before that it was just something we've always talked about, like our garret, that I really never believed would come true. I want you to know that I have, at this moment, 50 dollars saved for the great event. You have absolutely no idea of the privations I have suffered to put aside this trifle. I am walking to work to save gas money and have given up my $4 moisture cream and am using vaseline instead. But can I save enough for fall? Do you suppose they have a sail now, pay later plan? What if your school doesn't give you a leave? When would we go?

I've discovered that Elsie lionizes the "intellectuals" in town. She's always propelling me toward artistic types, convinced that if not taken under her wing I shall lead a dull and retarded life. Tonight it was a lecture by a sculptor named Santos Zingales who was very bored with it all and said he had ulcers. Last week it was an concert by the manic organist of the Presbyterian Church. The poor congregation is used to discreet musings from the loft as they file into their pews, but this organist assaults them with tremendous Bach toccatas and Buxte-something fugues. What thunderings, what unholy thoughts. Come to think of it, however, I have led rather a dull and retarded life these past months. No one seems to be waiting to give the gay divorcée a whirl. Over the hill at 22. Do you know that I am the first divorced person in my old crowd? Some of them haven't even married yet.

We did have an orgy the other night. Elsie has charmed a young Episcopalian priest and he dropped over for cocktails, stayed to dinner, and failed to leave after that. By nine o'clock Father John was attacking his second bottle of wine—flushed, rumpled and unbuttoned. Our room is lit only by firelight, wine and cocktail glasses are strewn about in abandon, the air is thick with cigarette smoke, and on the phonograph, at the good priest's request, throbs a torch song by Sarah Vaughan. I sit at his feet, unpenitent. There is a knock at the door. Come in, calls Elsie blithely, expecting Shep. In walks Reverend Manley from the Presbyterian Church on a Friday night recruiting mission. Father John staggers to his feet. Mother leads in Reverend Manley. He swallows hard, evidently forgeting the recruiting formula. He begins, chokes, turns to go. Mother shows him the door. Father John pours more wine. Obviously worrying about Presbyterians is beneath him. The orgy gathers steam.

The worldly priest and the cat-stroking boy upstairs are so far my only entertainment. The boy asked me whether I was a beatnik. I told him that if he'd ever heard me discussing children's vitamins over the fence with my neighbor he wouldn't ask such stupid questions.

Lawyer Berger continues to try to drum up grounds. He got me to admit that Jim had stayed locked in a closet with a young woman at a party for half an hour. "Surely you must have been suspicious, my dear: what do you think was going on all that time?" I wanted to say I'd been too busy in an adjacent bedroom to care, but didn't—he already accuses me of not taking the divorce seriously. Oh yes, I cried buckets the first time we went through the unhappy business, but ever since my eyes have been stones.

The other day I walked into Marc's room and there he was, pouring water from a milk bottle over his bed. He had a fleet of boats lined up on the blue cover. He looked at me with big blue eyes and said, "I'm trying to float them, Mama." The bed took days to dry.

When I start recounting my child's antics it's time to stop. Did I tell you how wonderful, even in newspaper reproduction, I thought your paintings were? I especially love "Moonlight Pond." You paint exactly to my taste and mood. So much energy. I'm dazzled.

Love, Jennie

*   *   *

Monday, April 16, 1956

Dear Jennie,

I write this with trepidation and penitence for having been quiet so long. I suppose you feel abandoned and angry and hurt, though I certainly hope not. It is just that in times of great trial I am incapable of writing a word, and these last weeks of getting the annual student art exhibit together have been weeks of hell.

I've discovered Mexico. Saw the bullfights, shopped, drank tequila, fought off the pimps and loose ladies, nightclubbed, climbed a mountain, and dragged north, broke physically and financially. Have to confess I got caught up in the color, the music and the excitement of the bullfights. The bull has no chance, of course, but it was satisfying to see a matador get gored, kicked in the skull, and carried out to thunderous olés.

My cat is lost. I wept for two days and then gave up both grieving and searching. He just walked out and never returned. Not a trace. Shan't get another.

Hurrah or alas! I'm not sure which, but I won't be back at Amarillo next year. No, I haven't been fired for seducing students or swearing at the dean: my predecessor didn't get his doctorate and is creeping back to old A.C. My demise seems to have affected me least of all. The students threaten mayhem, the faculty have got up a protest group, and even the administration seems genuinely sorry to part with such a gem. I know it's for the best.

Yet I have no idea what I'll be doing next year. Expect to summer again at Camp Mohawk, but after that all is veiled in mist. Haven't really started to look hard for jobs. Have a feeling that a Fulbright will come through. Besides, good things always seem to turn up and I guess I expect this to continue. Someday I may be rudely awakened.

The old fellow I share quarters with has become a decided nuisance. He tends to be too motherly, if that's what you call it, for my taste. When I go out he wants to know where I'm going, when I come in he wants to know where I've been. I have drawn an unspoken chalk line between my quarters and his, but it is always threatened. Fortunately it's April, or I'd have to give up this luxury and move on.

This is so important I wonder how I could forget it. Donald has married up. March 15 to someone named Mary Beth Dietman. I sent him congratulations. If only you had known about it you could have appeared at the ceremony heavily veiled and when the minister asked for objections, rushed down the aisle and thrown yourself upon Donald. He would have been enchanted. But seriously, I can't see him as a husband, can you? And what will they live on? He's never mentioned that he's employed. Maybe she's supporting him. Wonder whose running his father's business.

How is your novel? Send me more paragraphs, chapters, if you dare.

Take care of yourself, try to forgive my long silence, and don't go upstairs any more.

Rob

*   *   *

Thursday, May 3, 1956

Dear Rob,

I suppose I have to accept your frail excuse for your silence. Really. I hope you had a detestable time in Mexico. I'm glad your housemate is an old pervert. I'm glad your—no, not with the stoniest heart could I be glad that your little cat is gone. Now that I have railed and raged, you may bask in the balm of my forgiveness. You are probably asking, What have I done?

WHAT DO YOU MEAN (here I go again) "after that all is veiled in mist"? I thought we were going to Europe. What has happened to the Great Adventure? Week by week my little hoard grows. I've almost convinced Aunt Marie that Europe would be as educational as college for the fall. I'm saving "Holiday" articles. I'm wrestling with train schedules, luggage problems, short tours. Have you given up? No, no. I know your dauntless spirit. You will not fail me.

When I went to work at the Marathon Press, no one mentioned the bindery, a drear, drafty hall staffed by oafs. Imagine my horror when one day, because of the spring rush, I found myself among them. For eight hours I stood in one spot assembling invoices. Invoices have to be joggled. Joggling paper slices the hands. Paper cuts are unpleasant. By noon I had hundreds. My back ached, my shoulders ached. I wondered how I could get through the afternoon. At the end of the day I asked a colleague how long this exploitation of the secretarial help might go on. "Indefinitely," she said cheerfully.

The news about Donald almost made me cry. Who, I thought at first breath, would marry Donald. Old, inarticulate, hard-as-nails Donald. Then I thought of all his kindness to me over the years and thought: why, who wouldn't! Well, I wouldn't for one, but perhaps you know what I mean. I shall not send congratulations. Those days seem too far away and I haven't heard from Donald for years.

My aunt's old upright is now ensconced in the baronial dining room and I have unearthed all my old sheet music and am once more deep into "Pavane Pour Une Infante Defunte," the "Pathetique Sonata" and "Il Est Doux, Il Est Bon." I sing the latter to my accompaniment. Words cannot describe it.

Mark is getting smug and fat and draws endless pictures of "New York." Evidently the word fascinates him. His mother struggles with Chapter 21.

Must trot down to the bank to add another $5 to my Europe account. We are going, aren't we?

Love, Jennie

Postcards from Connor—Paris, Munich, Rome. Damn.

*   *   *

Thursday, May 10, 1956

Dear Jennie,

This promises to be a frantically busy summer for the Falkners. Item #1: Gingy is being married June 12. My father is planning a real extravaganza for her, despite the fact that it will probably land him in debtor's prison. He is convinced that "Annette would have wanted it this way," whereas my mother probably would have slipped them $500 to elope. The wedding will be in Milwaukee. Hope you can come. I'm due at Camp Mohawk shortly thereafter. Gingy has captured a nice fellow—looks, personality, and of all things, an art student. Dad frothed and raved for half a year, but Gingy is the kind of person who gets what she wants, and he finally consoled himself with the dim hope that two artists in the family may prove no worse than one. Gingy's all of 21 but plans on finishing her last year of college between making beds and putting up jelly.

New flash #2: I've got a Fulbright to study in Rome next year. Not much money but enough to furnish room, board, transportation and enough to see me through Europe and the Near East on holidays. I'm quite excited about the whole thing, especially about living on the edge of the Mediterranean in the cradle of civilization—if that makes good locational sense.

When shall we two meet again? Can you make the wedding? If not, shall I stop in Wausau on my way up to Mohawk? Then remember, there are all my golden days off during the eight weeks—perhaps now that you have a car you could come up to camp some day and bring Mark. I'll give you the grand tour. Bet Mark would love it. Please think about it.

Would love to hear your scintillating rendition of "Il Est Doux" accompanied by yourself on the old upright. Massenet is probably stirring somewhere under the sod.

Waiting for words—

Love, Rob

* * *

Thursday, June 14, 1956

Dear Jennie,

Am I abandoned or just neglected?

Almost called when I passed through Wausau, but your long and determined silence frightened me away.

Campers don't arrive till Friday. Meanwhile everyone fishes except Rob who seeks refuge in a biography of Stendahl.

Wedding was wonderful! Saw long-lost friends and relatives I had forgotten existed. Also saw Donald. He is under medical care. Said, bitterly, that after twenty years the doctor has discovered something wrong with his co-ordination. Also said that his father didn't really die of cancer—he put a gun in his mouth and pulled the trigger. The millions had somehow vanished: he was virtually bankrupt. Met Donald's wife. She is plain, dumpy, and didn't say a word. This will either make you laugh or cry: Donald is employed by the University as a maintenance man at Marietta House. Our Marietta House. Fate can certainly be grim.

Rob

*   *   *

Thursday, June 28, 1956

Dear Rob,

I didn't write after your letter of May 10 because—well, I couldn't. For one thing, the final divorce proceedings did me in. The lawyer really twisted the facts to come up with grounds: it sickened me. Of course Jim wasn't there. The divorce was uncontested—just me in a long-sleeved, dark grey dress trying to look injured when actually I was ecstatic to be free. I'd not like to go through that again. The alimony awarded is minimal, something like $52 a month. An insult, but I don't care. A year ago I would have sung and danced. Don't feel like that now.

Another reason for my silence was my bitter disappointment over the death of our European adventure. What's more, I've been going through a terrible ordeal with my family over you, all because I told them about our Europe plans and they jumped to conclusions. The whole lot expected this meant you were going to carry me away to the altar. They don't seem to be able to comprehend the situation. I've said nothing because there's nothing to say. I suppose they want to believe we'll marry, so they do. I've almost convinced Elsie of the facts by showing her your letter about Rome, but she still has lapses.

I know this is not clever nor subtle nor tactful, but if I must be clever, subtle or tactful with you, then all is hopeless.

Elsie is marrying Shep. He proposed last night. If you thought she looked young last summer, you should have seen her last night when she burst in with him—radiant in white. I am delighted, of course.

Well, Rob, do write. If you have a free afternoon, you know I'd love to see you. Fear not to be overwhelmed with cries of "Son!" And don't blame my family. They want me to be happy and get carried away. I shall protect you.

Love, Jennie

*   *   *

Thursday, July 19, 1956

Dear Jennie,

A hot, close, and crowded day, but now a very beautiful night. A gentle rain tapping at the roof, some timid thunder and shy lightning in the distance, and, most blessed of all, a soft breeze slipping through the cabin. Chopin is on the record player and my little tads are either asleep or pretending to be; so I balance my typewriter on my knees and write to you.

I hope you're not angry at either me or yourself for Thursday evening. Your demands were disturbing, insistent and very wonderful, and no matter what the eventualities, I shall always be grateful to you for making them. You have forced me to do some serious thinking for a change. Let us say it is high time.

I'm afraid that in trying to be kind I've been most selfish and cruel to you. I've sensed this but would never admit it, even to myself. I once hurt another person deeply, and in so doing wounded myself even more. Coward that I am, I've tried to avoid a repeat performance, but seem instead to have done the very thing I hoped most not to do.

Perhaps the kindest thing I could do would be to say "Let's stop writing. Let's stop seeing each other." But I'm not that generous, and call it love, friendship, or admiration, you have come to mean too much for me ever to take that step. You would have to make the break, and in doing so would take from me something which is so much a part of my life that I cannot imagine being without it. Of course, I want you to wait, but don't you see that I have no right to ask you. How can I expect you to sit at the hearthside while I go galloping around the world? But I will return, and I don't see how there could be anyone else but you.

I am not going to Rome to "test" you nor to escape you. This is something I've got to get out of my system. There have been many instances when I have known the turns my life would take before I ever reached them. Rome, or something similar, is inescapable. There is no great mystery about our relationship. It has been the story of a girl who grew up and a boy who refused to. At least, Jennie, he realizes this and, we hope, is growing. You would not have wanted him as he was, nor even as he is now.

Though you spoke of our "ephemeral" relationship, it strikes me that, on the contrary, it has been most enduring, despite troubled times. If I have been "cold" or "aloof" it is simply because I've always known that marriage would have to come later for me. How old are we—twenty-three? I think we have time. If you do love me and want me, you will have to wait. If you do not choose to, I can hardly blame you. I am grateful for your love, and you and Mark have mine.

If you want me to come Sunday I will. I will because I want to come . . . . It means as much to me as it does to you. I'll bring some records and some wine and we can be quiet and hidden.

I send you my love, my very durable love. Surely that is the best kind.

Rob

*   *   *

Friday, July 20, 1956

Dear Rob,

I've just finished War and Peace. It's three in the morning and I don't see how I'll go to work today, but of course I will. I could not put the book down, and not only because I fell madly, passionately in love with Prince Andrei.

I have put my own novel aside because I finally know that I know nothing about anything, including my heroine's trivial pains and joys and frustrations. I must find out about other lives before I go back to writing. I won't touch the typewriter again until I do.

I've made another vow. If I go back to school this fall I'm actually going to study. If I don't, I'm going to see the world. I don't know how, neither do I know why I'm telling you all this at this time of night.

I'll expect you Sunday, anytime, as soon as you can come. We will probably be deserted this weekend. Elsie and Shep are driving to Chicago, Aunt Marie is wheeling Grandmother to a family gathering. Incredibly, my terrorizing grandmother has lapsed into a deep and unbelievable senility. Plan on dinner here unless you distrust my culinary talents, in which case you can do the cooking.

I shall thank you properly for your letter then. Now I only send you my very durable love and laugh at your scruples about asking me to wait.

Has there ever been anyone else but you, Rob. Could there ever be.

Jennie

*   *   *

July 9, 1960

Dear Rob:

I was at Capitol and Murray, Donald was there, but where were you? At least I think Donald was there. I waited in my car fifteen minutes before I caught a glimpse in the rear-view mirror of a familiar figure with a crew cut crossing the street near the corner. By the time I'd pulled myself together enough to jump out of the car and run after him, he'd disappeared. I walked up and down the street for half an hour—combed the laundromats and grocery stores, then went back to my car (parked in plain view) and waited another half hour. Why did Donald insist on meeting on the corner anyway? Is he ashamed of his wife or something? Finally I drove off, heartbroken and cursing you both. What happened?

Perhaps you were there after all? I did see a white Ford parked on a side street. Could it have been yours? Impossible. Three adults could not converge on a Milwaukee street corner and miss each other—not even Rob Falkner, Donald Lindsay, and Jennie McAllister.

How could you not find me, Rob?

I was there.

Love, Jennie

Edwards Brothers, Inc.
Thorofare, NJ USA
May 26, 2011